10-MINUTE
BRAIN GAMES
BRAIN
TEASERS

About the Author

Dr. Gareth Moore is the internationally best-selling author of a wide range of brain-training and puzzle books for both children and adults, including *10-Minute Brain Games: Words and Language, 10-Minute Brain Games: Logic and Reasoning,* and *Brain Coach Intense.* His books have sold over a million copies and have been published in thirty different languages. He is also the creator of the online brain-training site BrainedUp.com and runs the daily puzzle site PuzzleMix.com.

10-MINUTE BRAIN GAMES

BRAIN TEASERS

Dr. Gareth Moore

imagine!

2022 First US edition
All rights reserved, including the right of reproduction in whole or in part
in any form. Charlesbridge and colophon are registered trademarks of
Charlesbridge Publishing, Inc.

At the time of publication, all URLs printed in this book were accurate and
active. Charlesbridge and the author are not responsible for the content or
accessibility of any website.

An Imagine Book
Published by Charlesbridge
9 Galen Street
Watertown, MA 02472
(617) 926-0329
www.imaginebooks.net

First published in Great Britain in 2021 by
Michael O'Mara Books Limited
9 Lion Yard
Tremadoc Road
London SW4 7NQ
Copyright © Michael O'Mara Books Limited 2021
Puzzles and solutions copyright © Gareth Moore 2021

ISBN 978-1-62354-552-9

Designed and typeset by Gareth Moore and Mira Kennedy

Printed in China
10 9 8 7 6 5 4 3 2 1

▪ Introduction ▪

Welcome to *10-Minute Brain Games: Brain Teasers*, packed from cover to cover with a huge range of challenging brain teasers.

Half of the brain teasers are written reasoning challenges, and half are logical grid puzzles—but one thing they all have in common is that there are never any gimmicks. All of the puzzles can be solved by careful step-by-step thought. There are no "cheat" answers in this book, where a puzzle is really some kind of wordplay riddle or in any way not what it appears to be.

If you are stuck, each of the written puzzles has a hint to help you solve it. The hints start on page 132.

Complete solutions are also included at the back of the book, starting on page 143, where the reasoning for each written puzzle is fully explained in a clear format. Some of these puzzles are reasonably straightforward, but others require much more careful thought—and for these it can be a genuine challenge simply to follow along fully with the solution, so if you are stuck it might well be worth reading the solution and then seeing if you can hide the solution and re-solve the puzzle yourself, based on what you have just read. It's not always as easy as it might sound!

The logical grid puzzles in the book cover a particularly wide range of relatively unusual types, so if at any point you aren't clear on the instructions for a particular puzzle, just flick to the back and take a look at its solution to see how it works. Then, when you're clear on the rules, return to the puzzle and start solving.

Good luck!

▪ Game of Gems ▪

Three sisters, Ruby, Amber, and Pearl, have each been gifted a pendant necklace by a rather quirky aunt. Each of the three necklaces has a single pendant attached.

The aunt gave one pendant containing a ruby, one containing amber, and one containing a pearl. She gifted them to her nieces in such a way that none of the girls was given the stone they actually share a name with.

"She was a strange woman, our Aunt Esmerelda," said Ruby.

"Absolutely," replied her sister, "since why on earth would she give me the pearl pendant necklace, when the alternative is so obvious?"

Which sister has the ruby pendant necklace?

Your solving time: _____

▪ **No Four in a Row** ▪

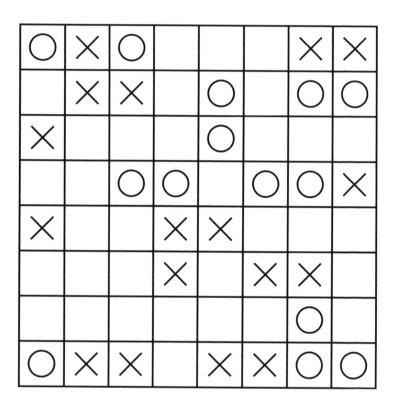

Instructions

Place either an "X" or an "O" into each empty square so
that no lines of four or more "X"s or "O"s are formed in any
direction, including diagonally.

Your solving time: _____

▪ The River Pets ▪

Three brothers—Ant, Ben, and Cal—are on their way home from a pet shop, each with a new pet. One has an owl, one has a cat, and one has a dog.

They come to a river on the way home, and there are three ways for them to cross it: a canoe, a kayak, and a raft. Each boy chooses a different boat to take him and his pet across:

- Only the canoe is big enough for the dog and its owner.
- Ben takes the kayak, and does not have an owl.
- Ant is not the brother who takes the raft.
- They all cross safely.

Who does the owl cross with, and in which type of boat?

Your solving time: _____   **9**

▪ Pizza Problem ▪

A man orders a pizza from his favorite restaurant over the phone. He tells the chef that he would like his pizza cut into eight slices, and that he will come and collect it at 8:00 p.m.

The chef knows that this particular customer is always late to collect his pizza. In order to encourage him not to be late, he tells the customer that his pizza will be ready in its box at 8:00 p.m. exactly, but that he will eat one slice of pizza from the customer's box every eight minutes, eating the first slice as soon as he knows the customer is late to collect it.

The customer eventually arrives at 8:34 p.m.

How many slices of pizza are left in the box?

Your solving time: _____

■ Meadows ■

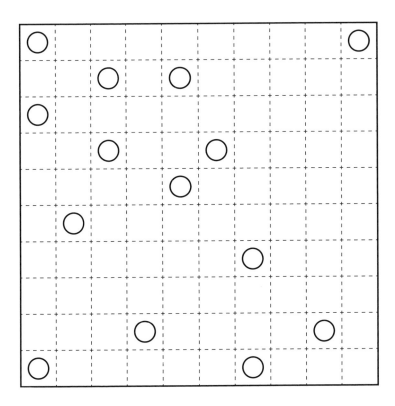

Instructions

Draw along the dashed lines to divide the grid into squares measuring 1×1 units or larger, with no unused areas left over.

• Every square must contain exactly one circle.

Your solving time: _____   **11**

▪ **Woolly Thinking** ▪

A grandmother decides that she will knit one woolly hat for each of her thirty grandchildren and wants to have them all ready in time for Christmas.

She knows she will have to knit two hats a week (starting from the day she decides to knit them) in order to have them all finished exactly on Christmas Eve, but she's sure she can get it done.

The grandmother knits away every day, not paying attention to the calendar. One day, however, she realizes that it's actually taking her one whole week to knit each hat, and she's only just managed to knit enough for half her grandchildren so far.

On what day does the grandmother have this realization?

Your solving time: _____

■ Dominoes ■

6	1	3	2	1	3	0	4
6	2	5	5	5	3	0	6
5	2	2	1	6	4	0	6
0	3	6	1	5	2	5	0
4	0	4	0	6	1	3	1
5	3	4	4	1	3	3	4
2	5	2	0	6	4	2	1

Instructions

Draw solid lines to divide the grid up to form a complete set of standard dominoes, with exactly one of each domino.

	0	1	2	3	4	5	6	
								0
								1
								2
								3
								4
								5
								6

- A "0" represents a blank on a traditional domino.
- Use the check-off chart to help you keep track of which dominoes you've placed.

Your solving time: _____

▪ Area Division ▪

H	A	F	B	G	D	B	H
D	C	F	B	D	F	E	G
G	C	A	H	H	C	C	A
D	A	E	D	G	E	C	A
A	B	F	D	G	C	H	E
B	F	H	E	A	B	F	G
C	E	H	C	G	B	A	B
H	G	E	F	E	D	D	F

Instructions
Draw along some of the dashed lines to divide the grid into a set of areas, each containing one of every letter from A to H.

Your solving time: _____

▪ Candy Selection ▪

A woman wants to buy jelly beans, so she visits a candy store.

The owner of the store shows the woman a large jar of jelly beans, which has a mix of thirteen different flavors inside, with an equal number of each flavor of bean.

The woman doesn't much mind which flavors she gets, but she has promised her four children she will give them each a jelly bean when she gets home. To prevent arguments, they must all have the same flavor. The sweet shop owner, however, says he does not let anyone choose individual jelly beans of particular flavors from the jar.

He says the woman may buy as many jelly beans as she likes, but they can't go back in the jar once he has taken them out.

The jelly beans cost a penny apiece.

What is the smallest number of pennies that the woman can spend in order to guarantee that she has at least four jelly beans of the same flavor?

▪ The Hat Trick ▪

Fifty prisoners are lined up and told that their prison is overcrowded, so some of them are to be released—and that they will each be given a fifty-fifty chance to win their freedom.

The prisoners stand in a single straight line, facing the backs of the prisoners ahead of them. They cannot see behind them.

A hat is placed on each prisoner, and the hat is always either red or green. No prisoner can see the hat they have been given, but they can see all the hats ahead of them.

The prison governor arrives, and announces that he will ask each prisoner which hat they have on. If they are correct, they will be allowed to leave the prison immediately. If they are wrong, they will have to serve the remainder of their sentence. They can only say one word, either "red" or "green," and nothing else.

He starts at the back of the line and then asks each prisoner in turn, working one by one from the back of the line to the front of the line.

If the prisoners had been given a chance to confer before being given their hats, could they have come up with a strategy which would improve their odds above fifty-fifty?

With the best possible strategy, how many of the fifty prisoners could be guaranteed to win their freedom?

Your solving time: _____

■ Entries and Exits ■

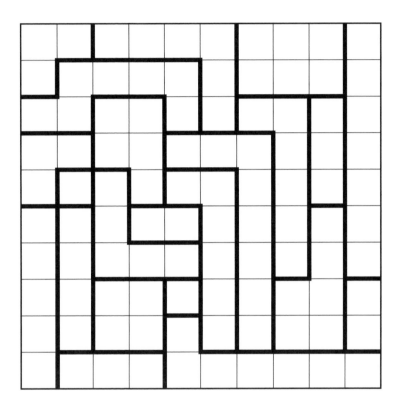

Instructions

Draw a loop that visits every square.

- The loop should only travel horizontally or vertically and cannot visit any square more than once.
- The loop can only enter and exit each bold-lined region once.

Your solving time: _____

▪ Loop Finder ▪

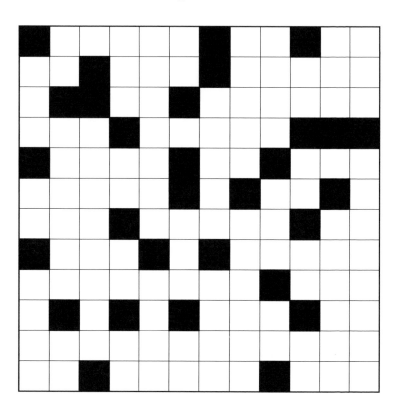

Instructions

Draw a single loop that visits every white square exactly once.

- The loop cannot touch or cross over either itself or a black square at any point.
- The loop consists only of horizontal and vertical line segments.

Your solving time: _____

▪ The Vanishing Money ▪

A restaurant bill arrives and the total is $30. A party of three people have been dining, and they each pay $10.

Shortly after the party has paid, the waiter arrives and apologizes. The bill was incorrect, and in fact the total amount owed should have been $25, not $30.

On explaining this mistake, the waiter proposes that, as it would be impossible to perfectly divide the $5 owed among the three people, he should give them each $1 back and keep $2 as a tip.

The party agrees to the above suggestion, but as they are about to leave, one of them exclaims loudly:

"Wait a moment! We have all now each paid $9, and you have also kept $2—but this gives a total of only $29! What has happened to the remaining dollar, to make up the original total of $30?"

What indeed? Can you explain the missing dollar?

▪ The Tournament ▪

Lancelot, Gawain, and Percival were taking part in a jousting tournament in the arena within the gardens of Camelot. As there were only three of them, they decided to organize the tournament so that the winner of each match would remain in the jousting arena and continue to play the knight who had not taken part in the previous match.

Lancelot had to miss one match to change his horse after the first nine matches had been completed, as he had jousted in all of them and his horse was tired.

At the end of the day, they counted up the various matches they had all jousted in. There had been fifteen matches in total:

• Lancelot had jousted in twelve matches.
• Gawain had jousted in seven matches.
• Percival had jousted in eleven matches.

Who jousted in the fourteenth match of the day, and who won that match?

Your solving time: _____

▪ Gaps ▪

	1	1	1	1	1	1	7	3	3
1									
1									
1									
1									
2									
1									
2									
1									
1									

Instructions

Shade two squares in every row and column, so that the number of unshaded squares between those two squares is equal to the number at the start of the corresponding row or column.

• Shaded squares do not touch, not even diagonally.

Your solving time: _____

21

▪ Shape Fit ▪

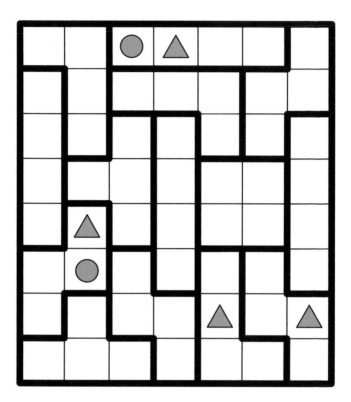

Instructions

Place circles and triangles into some squares so every bold-lined region contains exactly one circle and exactly one triangle. Two identical shapes cannot be in touching grid squares—not even diagonally.

Your solving time: _____

▪ Paintball Probabilities ▪

An opportunity has arisen for just one employee of a particular bank to spend a week on a beautiful, tropical island as part of a business deal.

Three bankers, Oli, Jen, and Laila, all want to go on the trip, and they decide to settle the matter by having a competition at the local paintball range. The competition will involve the three participants taking turns to fire a paintball, with each taking a single shot on their turn. Anyone who is hit will be eliminated from the competition, and the last person remaining will go on the trip.

The three colleagues have jointly calculated how likely they are to hit their target. Oli has the worst aim of them all, with only a one in three chance of accurately hitting his mark. Jen is the next best, with a two in three chance. Laila is the most accurate shooter of the three, with a 100 percent success rate.

They decide that Oli will take his shot first, followed by Jen, then Laila. Oli will then take his second turn if he has not already been eliminated, and the circle will continue in this manner until everyone has been eliminated except for one. Each of the participants wants to go on the trip and will follow the strategy that they believe gives them the best chance of winning.

What strategy would give Oli the best chance of going on the trip to the tropical island?

_____

_____

■ An Umbrella for Two ■

Four family members are sitting in a railway station's waiting room. In order to reach their required platform, they must travel outside for a distance. The waiting room and the platform are both sheltered from the elements, but it is raining heavily outside and the route between them is open to the elements.

The four people—Marcel, Dani, Lola, and Zara—wish to reach the platform without getting wet but have only one umbrella between them. The umbrella is able to keep up to two people dry at a time, but naturally only if these two people walk together at the same speed. Since the four of them have different walking speeds, the fastest in each pair will need to slow down and move at the speed of the slowest of the pair when sharing the umbrella.

They estimate that their fastest times to reach the platform will be as follows:

• Marcel: one minute
• Dani: two minutes
• Lola: seven minutes
• Zara: ten minutes

Their train arrives in seventeen minutes. How can they all reach the platform in time, without anyone getting wet?

Your solving time: _____

■ Every Second Turn ■

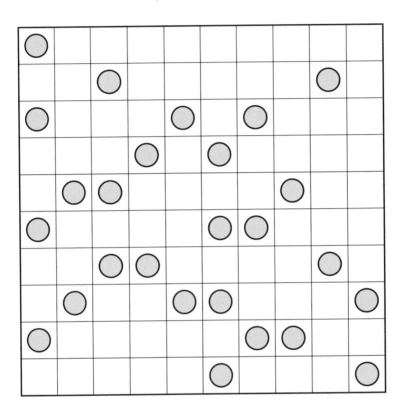

Instructions

Draw a loop that visits every square exactly once, consisting of horizontal and vertical lines between squares.

• Every second turn on the loop is indicated by a circle.

Your solving time: _____

■ The Professor's Children ■

Two university professors were eating in their college dining room one evening when conversation turned to their families. The first professor told the other that he has three children. The second professor then asked how old these children were.

The first professor was feeling mischievous, and replied, "The product of my three children's ages is seventy-two. The sum of their ages is the same as the current day of the month."

The second professor checked which day of the month it was, but declared that he was still unable to work out the ages of the three children.

"I'll give you some more information, then," said the first professor, "so you can be certain of their ages: my eldest child is the captain of her school football team."

How old are the three children?

Your solving time: _____

▪ Shape Link ▪

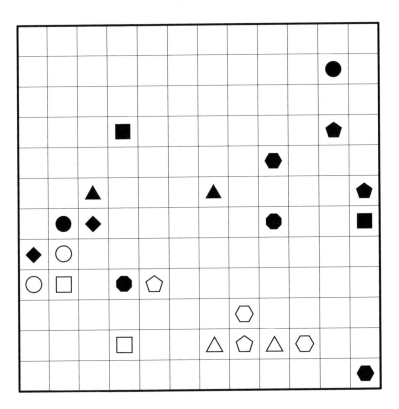

Instructions

Draw a series of separate paths, each connecting a pair of identical shapes.

- No more than one path can enter any square.
- Paths can only travel horizontally or vertically between squares.

Your solving time: _____   27

▪ Arrow Maze ▪

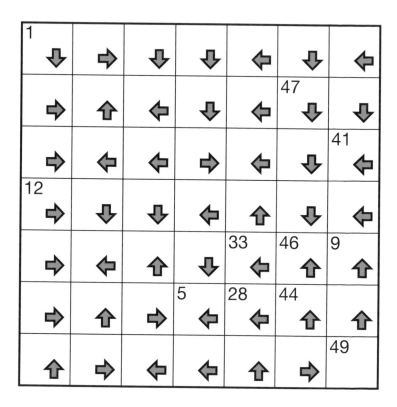

Instructions

Add numbers to the grid so that every square contains a number, and each number from 1 to 49 appears exactly once.

• Every number must be in a square with an arrow that points in the precise direction of the next highest number.

Your solving time: _____

▪ Paper Chains ▪

You have decided to throw a garden party for some friends. To make your garden look more festive, you decorate one of your trees using paper chains.

You have eight short paper chains in your box of decorations, each consisting of seven paper loops. To decorate the tree, you want to join the eight individual chains together into a single continuous circular chain, consisting of fifty-six paper loops.

Your brother and sister are helping you to decorate the tree, and your brother tells you that you need to break and reseal eight paper loops in order to join the chains together and create the long circular loop. Your sister disagrees, saying you can do it by breaking and resealing seven loops.

Who is correct? What is the minimum number of loops you would need to break and reseal in order to create a circular chain of fifty-six connecting loops?

▪ **Binary Puzzle** ▪

				0		1	
					1		
		0		0			
						1	
0					1		0
0				0		1	
	1			0			
	1						

Instructions

Place a 0 or 1 in every empty square so that there is an equal number of each digit in every row and column.

• Reading along a row or column, there may be no more than two of the same digit in succession.

Your solving time: _____

▪ Team-Building ▪

A group of company employees are out together for a day of team-building exercises led by an expert instructor.

The instructor divides the group into two teams and names them team A and team B. Team A has seven employees, each of whom is given a chair. The instructor organizes team A so that their chairs are positioned in a circle, and they are all sitting on their respective chairs. She then tells the remaining employees, who make up team B, that their job is to create a situation where all of the employees in team A are simultaneously standing.

Employees in team B can only make employees in team A change between sitting and standing, or vice versa, by tapping them on the shoulder. Every time a shoulder is tapped, not only the person tapped but also the person immediately to their left and the person immediately to their right must change state—so if they were standing before, they must sit; and if they were sitting before, they must now stand.

What is the minimum number of shoulder taps needed to reach a situation where everyone in team A is standing up?

Your solving time: _____   31

▪ The Corridor ▪

A game-show host decided to test the reasoning abilities of her contestants by introducing a new challenge to the show.

The premise was simple: there were five doors at the back of the studio numbered 1-5 in order, each leading onto the same corridor. The game show host sent her assistant into the corridor and told him to choose a door to stand behind, out of sight of the contestants. The contestants were then asked to guess which door the assistant was standing behind.

After they had guessed, the host opened that door to reveal if her assistant was behind it or not, and then shut it again if they were wrong.

Each time a door was shut, the assistant would move exactly one door to the left or to the right of their current position at random. Of course, if they were at doors 1 or 5 they did not have a choice and would have to move to doors 2 or 4, respectively.

What is the minimum number of guesses that is required to be certain of finding the assistant? What strategy should be used?

Your solving time: _____

■ Train Tracks ■

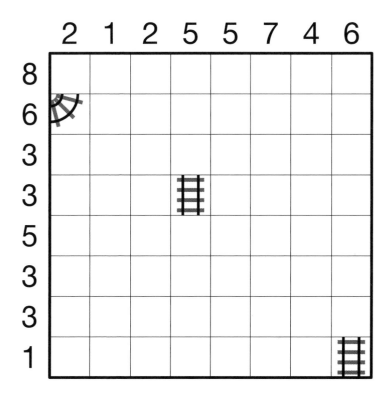

Instructions
Draw track pieces in some squares to complete a track that travels all the way from its entrance in the leftmost column to its exit in the bottom row.

- The track can't otherwise exit the grid, and it cannot cross itself.
- Numbers outside the grid reveal the number of track pieces in each row and column.
- Every track piece must either go straight or turn a right-angled corner.

Your solving time: _____   33

▪ Line Sweeper ▪

	0					4		2
2	2	4						
		6			3			
		7			3			
	5							5
	6							
			5					

Instructions

Draw a single loop that passes through some of the empty squares, using horizontal and vertical lines.

- The loop cannot re-enter any square.
- The loop must pass through the given number of touching squares next to each number clue, including diagonally touching squares.

Your solving time: _____

■ The Prizes ■

A professor decided to test a group of ten students on their reasoning ability. She took ten pieces of paper and wrote the word "apple" on each, then folded them up and gave one each to the students.

"I have written the name of a piece of fruit on each piece of paper," she told the students, "but you may *not* read your own piece of paper. However, you may read what is written on the paper of any other student, with the condition that you do not reveal the information you have learned.

"At least one of you has the word 'apple' written on your paper. If you think that *you* have the word 'apple,' you may come up to me directly at the end of a lecture and tell me so. If you are right, I will give you a prize. But if you are wrong, you will fail this course."

The students were rule-abiding, so none of them looked at their own paper, but they also wanted to win a prize and not risk failing their course. They all read every other student's piece of paper, but none of them revealed any information to their classmates, and they all attended every class for the rest of the term. At the end of the tenth class, all ten students asked the professor for a prize—and received it.

How had they all managed to work out what was on their own piece of paper without looking at it?

Your solving time: _____

▪ Clouds ▪

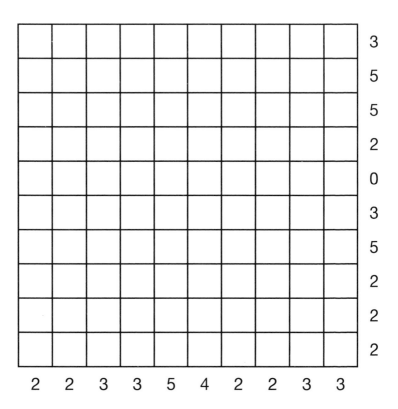

Instructions

Shade rectangular groups of grid cells, such that each group is at least two cells wide and at least two cells tall.

- Rectangular groups of cells cannot touch, not even diagonally.
- Given number clues specify the number of shaded cells in each row and column.

Your solving time: _____

■ Competitive Cake ■

A bakery ran a competition whereby customers could win a free cake if they managed to solve a logical challenge.

Each customer taking part in the challenge was blindfolded and sat in front of a square cake stand. The head baker then placed four ramekins on the stand, one in each corner. Each of the ramekins was placed either upside down or the right way up, but the customer did not know which was which since they were blindfolded.

The customer then had the chance to choose any two ramekins and feel with their hands to work out whether they were upside down or the right way up. They could then turn over one or both of the ramekins, or leave them as they were. After this decision had been made, the head baker rotated the cake stand by some multiple of 90 degrees. Then, the process repeated with the customer once again able to choose two ramekins to feel, and so on.

Any customer who managed to get all of the ramekins to face either upside down or the right way up at the same time in five turns or fewer would win the cake. The head baker would tell the customer if they had been successful or not after each turn.

What strategy could be used to guarantee winning the cake?

_____

_____

▪ Mowing Matters ▪

Two gardeners, Olivia and Remi, were employed to mow fifty lawns that belonged to a row of fifty houses on the same street. To make their job more interesting, they decided to organize a competition. They agreed that whichever gardener mowed the final lawn, of the fiftieth house, would be the winner.

Only one of them would mow each day, and each gardener was able to mow a maximum of ten lawns in a day but could choose to mow fewer, so long as they mowed at least one and fully completed each lawn they mowed. No lawn could be mowed more than once.

Olivia was confident that she would be the one to mow the fiftieth lawn, since it had been agreed that she could choose whether to go first or second.

Should she choose to go first or second? What is her method to guarantee she gets to be the one to mow the fiftieth lawn?

Your solving time: _____

▪ Loop the Loop ▪

```
    3       3       3 2 3 2 3
  3     1     1       3 2 3 2
    3       0     0 1     2 2
  3 1     0     1     3     2
  3           1 3 1     3 3
  2 0     0 2 2             1
  1     0     3     2     3 3
  2 3     0 3     3     2
  2 2 1 1     1     1     1
  3 2 2 1 3     3     1
```

Instructions

Connect some of the dots to create a single loop, so that each digit has the specified number of adjacent line segments.

- Dots can only be joined by horizontal or vertical lines.
- Each dot can be used no more than once.

Your solving time: _____   39

▪ **Star Battle** ▪

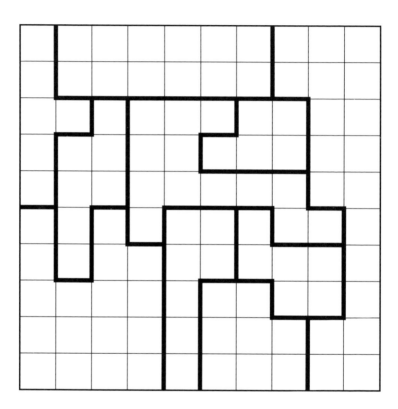

Instructions

Place stars in some squares so that each row, column, and outlined region contains exactly two stars.

• Stars cannot touch each other—not even diagonally.

Your solving time: _____

■ Emerald Erudition ■

Two jewelers were waiting for opening time at their jewelry shop, and decided to play a game with five standard dice.

The first jeweler said to the other, "I will roll this set of five dice five times. At the same time as each roll, I will design a set of emerald-and-diamond rings in my head. These rings will all have a certain number of emeralds set around a central diamond. I will say aloud to you how many emeralds in total are in each set of imaginary rings. My decision-making process will follow a pattern, so all you have to do is work out what that pattern is."

The first jeweler rolled the dice, while the second watched closely. The numbers in the first roll were 1, 2, 3, 3, and 5. The second roll gave a 2, 3, 4, 4, and 5. The third roll produced a 1, 3, 3, 6, and 6. In the fourth roll, the result was 2, 2, 3, 5, and 6. In the fifth roll, the dice showed 2, 2, 3, 3, and 5.

After each roll, the first jeweler gave the number of emeralds in each set of rings she had designed. For the first set of rings, she used 8 emeralds. She used 6 for the second set, and 4 for the third set. For the fourth set, she used 6, and in the fifth set she used 8.

What rule corresponding to the dice rolls was she following to design her rings?

Your solving time: _____   **41**

▪ Up and Down ▪

A woman receives the following text message from her husband:

Hope I'm not interrupting, but I need your help with something—I'm having a bit of a meltdown at home. I was looking in the cupboard this morning for the summer quilt and could only find that enormous eiderdown, which is no good in this heat. I might be being stupid but do you remember where I said I'd put it? It must either be in the attic or the downstairs closet. It's the handmade one—really super-quality embroidery—and I'm sure I didn't get it down from the attic last year, although I suppose I might have taken it to the dry cleaners after that soup incident. I've been looking in both places all morning and I'm not sure that attic ladder will support another trip up. Sorry to be abrupt, but can you give me a call?

Where does the message suggest the husband has spent the most of his time searching: up in the attic or down in the closet? The husband has subconsciously embedded a series of hints to help answer this question.

Your solving time: _____

▪ Yin Yang ▪

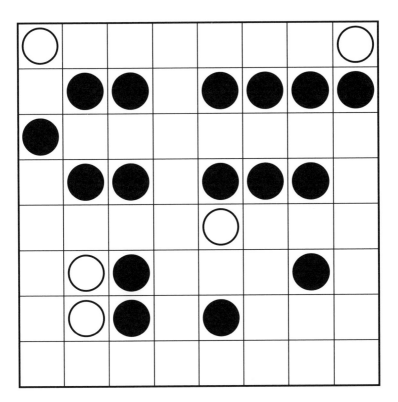

Instructions

Every empty square must have either a black or a white circle added to it. All circles of the same color must form a single continuous region, where you can travel from any circle of that color to any other of the same color while stepping only via circles of that color.

- Steps can only be horizontally or vertically between touching squares.
- There may not be any 2×2 areas of the same color.

Your solving time: _____

▪ **Castle Wall** ▪

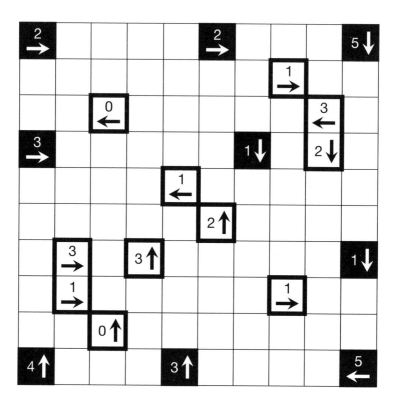

Instructions

Draw a loop that travels between the centers of some touching empty squares using only horizontal and vertical lines, without revisiting any square.

- All white clues must be within the loop, and all black clues outside the loop.
- Clue squares show the total length in square widths of all loop segments running in the directions shown.

Your solving time: _____

▪ Soup Selection ▪

A chef has made soup for a special event in his restaurant. Over ten liters of soup had been prepared in a large cooking vessel, but he knew that exactly eight liters were needed to feed all of the guests, and he wanted to save the rest of the soup to feed the waiters.

He had planned to measure this out exactly using an industrially sized measuring jug, but he discovered that one of the other chefs had broken this jug, and so all he had to measure out the quantity of soup was a ten-liter tureen and a six-liter serving bowl. The only marking on both the bowl and the tureen was their capacity, so it was impossible to measure exactly eight liters using either of them alone.

How could the chef measure exactly eight liters of soup, without wasting any? Assume he is capable of lifting and pouring the soup without spilling any.

Your solving time: _____

▪ Bridges ▪

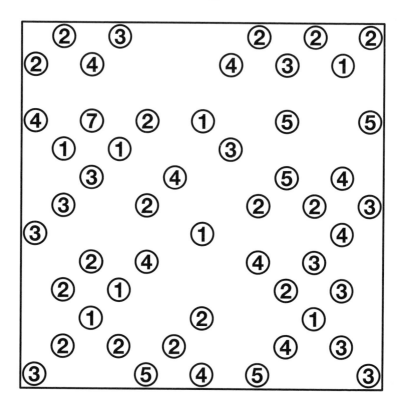

Instructions

Join circled numbers with horizontal or vertical lines. Each number must have as many lines connected to it as specified by its value.

- No more than two lines may join any pair of numbers, and no lines may cross.
- The finished layout must connect all numbers, so you can travel between any pair of numbers by following one or more lines.

Your solving time: _____

• Incense-ative Problem •

A church deacon spent every Saturday afternoon preparing for the Sunday service. She had become accustomed to spending two hours cleaning before taking a thirty-minute break to sit on one of the pews and enjoy the peaceful atmosphere. She always used the large clock above the church door to time her break.

One afternoon, the clock stopped while she was cleaning. She was unsure how she was going to time her thirty-minute break, but then remembered that there were some incense sticks in one of the church cupboards that she might be able to use to help her.

These incense sticks had been gifted to the church by a local shopkeeper who made the incense sticks himself. They were slender bamboo sticks coated in incense paste which could be lit from either end. The shopkeeper had proudly told the deacon that he used an exact amount of paste on each stick, meaning that each stick took exactly forty minutes to burn from one end to the other before going out. However, the incense paste was thicker in some places than others on the different sticks, so although each stick burned for exactly forty minutes each, different sections of the sticks burned at different rates. For example, half of one stick might be burned in ten minutes, then it would take thirty minutes to burn through the rest.

How could the deacon use two of these irregularly burning incense sticks to measure her thirty-minute break?

▪ Year by Year ▪

Two historians were playing a game in which they had to guess a year anywhere between the years 1 and 2000 AD. One of the historians would think of a date, and the other would ask a series of questions to ascertain the year they were thinking of.

These questions could each be answered in one of three ways:

- "That year is correct."
- "That year is too early."
- "That year is too late."

The first historian announced that they had thought of a year, and the second historian considered their strategy. After thinking for a minute, they announced to their friend that they were certain that they could always guess the year correctly within a particular number of guesses.

In the worst-case scenario, how many guesses would they need?

Your solving time: _____

■ Lasers ■

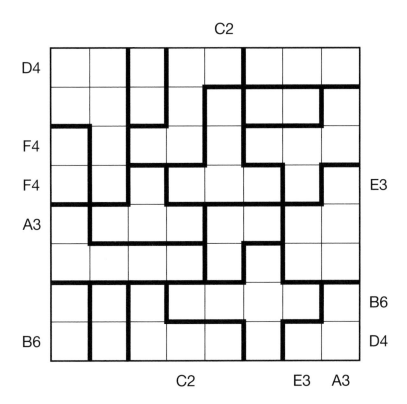

Instructions

Draw diagonal lines across certain squares to form mirrors, with exactly one mirror per bold-lined region.

• The mirrors must be placed so that a laser fired perpendicularly into the grid from each lettered clue would then exit the grid at the same letter elsewhere, having bounced off the exact number of mirrors indicated by the number next to the letter.

Your solving time: _____   **49**

▪ Cattle Call ▪

A dairy farmer wanted to build up his herd of cows. He thought for a while about how best to achieve this, and eventually decided that each of his breeding cows could be allowed to have as many female calves as it wanted until such time as it bore its first male calf. At that point he would permanently keep it away from the bulls, to stop it from having any more calves.

His plan would therefore ensure that no female cow had more than one male calf, but could have any number of female calves. He reasoned that therefore over time the proportion of female to male animals in his herd would increase.

Is the farmer correct? Assume that all cows have an even chance of giving birth to either a female or a male calf.

Your solving time: _____

■ Multi Loops ■

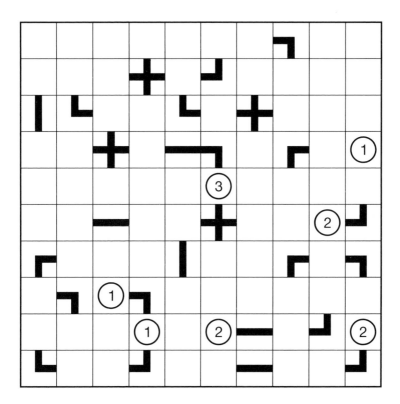

Instructions

Draw a set of loops that together pass through all squares, so at least one loop visits every square of the grid. In each square a loop may pass straight through, turn 90 degrees, or cross directly over another loop segment.

- Apart from in crossing squares, only one loop may enter any one square.
- Lines can never be drawn diagonally.
- Each loop must pass through at least one circle, and all circles with the same number must be part of the same loop and no other. Squares with given loop segments cannot be changed.

Your solving time: _____   **51**

■ Minesweeper ■

			3				
2		2			5		3
	2			4		3	
1			4			5	
	3		5				1
			5			3	
		3		4			1
1	1	1	2		2		1

Instructions
Place mines into some empty squares in the grid. Clues in some squares show the number of mines in touching squares—including diagonally.

• No more than one mine may be placed per square.

Your solving time: _____

▪ Safe Solution ▪

A pair of thieves were attempting to break into a safe in the study of a wealthy art collector, in which they knew he stored some valuable jewelry.

They were experienced in the art of breaking into most models of safe, but they found that this particular model was a state-of-the-art design that couldn't be broken open with the tools they carried with them.

The thieves decided that their only strategy would be to enter the correct code into the safe, and they started searching the office to see if the art collector had written the code down. The code to the safe could have any number of digits, making narrowing down the options a daunting task.

After searching for some minutes, they found a piece of paper with "safe code = next number in sequence" written at the top in pencil, with a series of numbers beneath:

5   15   1115   3115   132115

Which number should the thieves enter into the safe? It is the immediately following number in the sequence shown.

Your solving time: _____

▪ No Change ▪

William was visiting London and wanted to buy a snack from a vending machine, but when he checked his wallet, he realized that he did not have any change, and the smallest coin he could find was £1. He asked a passer-by if he had any change for a pound.

"Sorry, I'm afraid I don't," replied the passer-by. "And in fact I don't even have the change to break up a 50-pence, 20-pence, 10-pence, or 5-pence coin."

"Goodness. You must be completely out of change then," William observed.

"Oh no," the man said, "I have £1.43 in my wallet. I just can't give you smaller coins that add up exactly to any of these amounts."

Keeping in mind that British money has coins worth a penny and 2 pence, as well as the denominations mentioned above, exactly which coins, and how many of each, did the passer-by have in his wallet?

Your solving time: _____

▪ Easy as A, B, C, D ▪

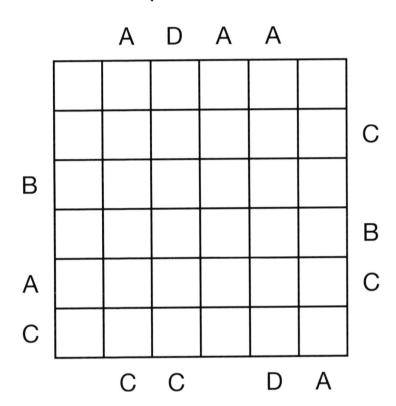

Instructions

Place A, B, C, and D once each into every row and column within the grid. This means that there will be one empty square in every row and column.

- Each letter given outside the grid must match the closest letter to it in within the same row/column.
- Letters may not share squares.

Your solving time: _____   55

■ Skyscrapers ■

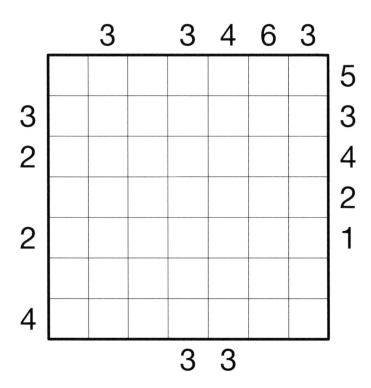

Instructions

Place a digit from 1 to 7 into every square, so that no digit repeats in any row or column inside the grid.

• Each clue number outside the grid gives the number of digits that are "visible" from that point, looking along that clue's row or column. A digit is visible unless there is a higher digit preceding it, reading from the clue along the row or column. E.g., in "2143576" the 2, 4, 5, and 7 are visible from the left, but 1 is obscured by the 2; 3 is obscured by the 4; and 6 is obscured by the 7—so its clue would be "4."

Your solving time: _____

▪ A Narrow Path ▪

An architectural practice had been commissioned to build a spherical building, set into the ground so that exactly half of the sphere is visible above the ground. The circumference of the sphere would be exactly 2,500 meters.

All went to plan with the build, and for the grand opening of the building the architects decided to tie a long ribbon around the building at ground level. They ordered a 2,500-meter-long ribbon that would fit snugly around the circumference of the sphere, with ends that could be attached together to make a continuous loop. However, when the ribbon arrived, they found that it was five meters longer than planned.

One of the architects suggested arranging the ribbon so it was pulled away from the building, to form a circular path between the building and the ribbon.

"But no one will be able to walk along such a path! Surely its width would be too small?" exclaimed one of the architects.

Assuming the ribbon was arranged so that it was exactly the same distance away from the building at all points, how wide would the path between the building and the ribbon be? Could you walk between it and the building?

Your solving time: _____

▪ Inbetweener ▪

	7			7	2	6	
	7	7	5		2		
1	5		5			6	
		5		3	5		
	4		6	1			4
5	1	6	6		1	4	2

Instructions

Draw along the grid lines to divide all of the grid into regions, so every region contains two numbers.

• Each region must contain a number of grid squares that is strictly between the value of the two numbers. So if the numbers are 5 and 12, then the region must contain between six and eleven squares.

Your solving time: _____

■ Apple Rows ■

Two customers, Oli and Gwen, were arguing at a market fruit stall. The fruit-seller only had one pineapple left, and both of them wanted to take it home. To establish who would get the pineapple, the fruit-seller came up with a game.

She took nine apples out of a box and arranged them into three rows: two apples on the top row, three apples on the middle row, and four apples on the bottom row.

She then told Oli and Gwen that they should take turns removing one or more apples, but that all of the apples they removed on each turn had to come from the same row. The customer who took the final apple would win, and get to take home the pineapple.

The customers flipped a coin to decide who would go first. Gwen won the toss and decided to go first, knowing that she could guarantee her victory.

Which apples should Gwen take first in order to be sure of winning the pineapple?

▪ Hairy Situation ▪

Two hairdressers were chatting to each other while they worked. Conversation came around to their children, and in particular the color of their children's hair.

One of the hairdressers was known for her roundabout way of describing things, so when she began describing the color of her children's hair, her colleague's heart sank. Rather than saying outright how many children she had and what color each of their hair was, she instead told the second hairdresser:

"All but two of my children have red hair, all but two have light-brown hair, and all but two have dark-brown hair."

How many children did the hairdresser have?

Your solving time: _____

▪ Fences ▪

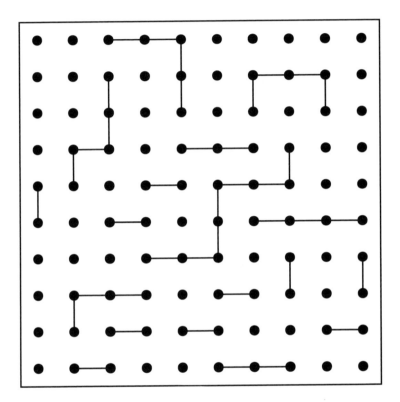

Instructions

Join all of the dots to form a single loop.

- The loop does not cross over or touch itself at any point.
- The loop can only consist of horizontal and vertical lines between dots.

▪ **Snake** ▪

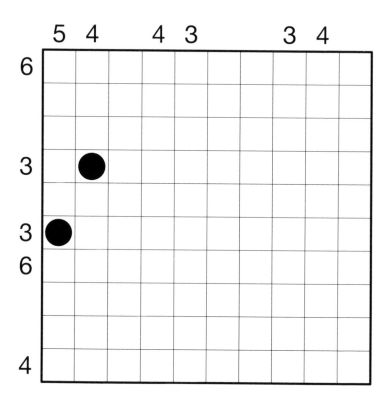

Instructions

Shade some squares to form a single snake that starts and ends at the squares marked with circles.

- A snake is a path of adjacent squares that does not branch or cross over itself.
- The snake does not touch itself—not even diagonally, except when turning a corner.
- Numbers outside the grid reveal the number of squares in their row or column that contain part of the snake.

Your solving time: _____

• Bus Numbers •

Katherine decided to go to the beach one weekend and caught a bus to the nearest seaside town. However, as she lived a long way from the beach, it was a four-hour bus journey.

She settled into her seat and watched the various vehicles traveling in the opposite direction throughout the long journey.

As she watched, she spotted a bus with the same number as hers going in the opposite direction, back towards where she lived.

Some quick internet research told her that buses on this route departed from the beach once every hour.

How many buses on the same route would Katherine expect to see in total throughout her journey, other than the one she was traveling on?

Your solving time: _____

▪ Pipeline ▪

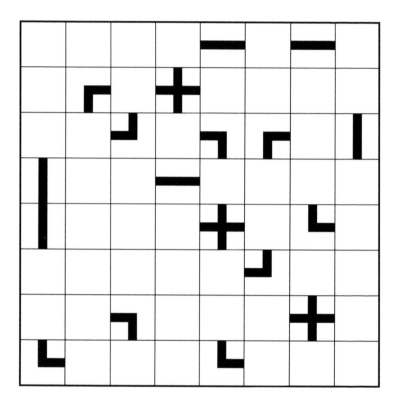

Instructions

Draw either a straight line, a corner, or a crossing segment in each empty square in order to form a single loop that visits every square.

- The loop may only travel horizontally or vertically between square centers.
- Some parts are given, and cannot be changed.

Your solving time: _____

▪ Coat Color Challenge ▪

Two customers have each delivered nine winter coats to a dry-cleaning shop. Each customer has sent three blue coats, three red coats, and three black coats: eighteen coats in total. The coats are identical apart from their colors, and are promptly labeled and hung up on two different racks, one rack per customer.

Since it was a quiet day, the staff at the dry cleaners, Jon and Joe, decided to play a game.

Joe blindfolded Jon and then rearranged the order of the coats on each rack, so Jon could not use his memory to work out what color each coat was. He then told Jon to take as many coats as he could from the first customer's rack, while leaving sufficiently few coats that there was certain to be at least one coat of each color on the first rack.

Next, Joe hung the removed coats in random places on the second rack, so Jon did not know which was which. He then asked Jon, who was still blindfolded, to take some coats from the second coat rack and hang them back on the first rack. However, Jon's challenge was to take the smallest possible number of coats that would guarantee at least two coats of each color would be hanging on the first rack once he had finished.

Assuming Jon fulfilled both parts of his challenge, how many coats were on the second coat rack at the conclusion of the game?

_____

_____

▪ The Value of Reading ▪

A library was having a book sale in order to create space for new stock. In order to save the library from having lots of change at the end of the day, the librarian had made sure every book on sale had a price that was an exact multiple of a dollar. To keep the pricing simple, all books were classified as either reference, nonfiction, or fiction for the purposes of the sale.

As well as selling books, the head librarian had set up a book exchange corner where people could come and swap books which they had finished for new ones that they hadn't read. This could be done on the same value basis that was being used for the book sale, so if one type of book was twice as expensive as another, then you would need two of that other type to exchange for one of the more expensive type.

The librarian had written a sign that read: "Exchange rate: five reference books for six nonfiction books, or two reference books and three nonfiction books for nine fiction books." Next to it, he had written a separate sign that made it clear that you could buy three fiction books and two nonfiction books for a total price of nineteen dollars.

What were the individual sales prices of a single reference book, nonfiction book, and fiction book?

_____

_____

Your solving time: _____

▪ **Walls** ▪

	7				6			
		3		3				1
2				5		5		
								1
	6		3		2		5	
1								
		4		5				3
3				3		5		
			2				4	

Instructions

Draw a horizontal or vertical line across the full width or height of the center of every white square.

- The total length of all lines touching each black square must be equal to the number printed on that cell.
- The length of a line is defined as the number of squares it covers.
- Some lines may be shared between black squares; other lines may not touch any black squares.

Your solving time: _____   67

▪ **Four Winds** ▪

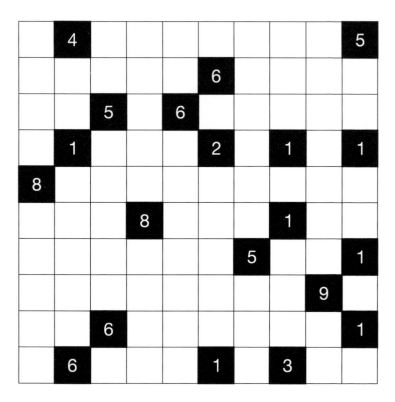

Instructions

Draw one or more horizontal or vertical lines emanating from each numbered square.

- Lines cannot cross numbered squares or enter the same square as another line.
- Each number indicates how many squares its lines travel into; the numbered squares themselves are not counted.
- All squares must be visited by a line.
- Each line can only connect to a single number.

Your solving time: _____

■ Family Confusion ■

The food had been finished at the Redwood family Christmas dinner, and some members of the family had begun to play games.

In order to help keep the children amused, Uncle Peter had devised some questions that would test their logical thinking.

He started by giving the children three seemingly unmathematical statements that they could use to work out the solution:

- $7 + 6 = 1$
- $6 + 8 = 2$
- $4 + 11 = 3$

"Despite first appearances, all of these sums make sense when using a particular system that you should all know well," he told the bewildered children. "Can you work out what that system is, and then tell me the answer to $9 + 5$?"

What is the system, and what would be the answer to his sum?

• Task Force Task •

A letter arrives:

You have, to date, been a model task force operative, and we need your assistance with a serious but sensitive matter. You will receive a series of important and confidential memos; carry on with your other work, but pay attention to concealed messages. Once the investigation has officially begun, I—for my own safety—will be moved to a secret location. For the duration of this operation you have been given the codename Cobra, voted for by your superiors. An "employee" who claims to work for us has managed to obtain confidential images and documents that pertain to top-secret missions. The chosen method of smuggling information from our premises seems to involve some kind of radio code.

The final facts of the matter are still unclear to us, so we need your help. We would like you to begin by looking into unusual transactions made in the company name at golf courses across the country. We chose you because we believe you stand the best chance of success, given your attention to detail. We are hoping to have the operation wrapped up by early November. Can you discover where the charlatan got his information?

What secret two-word message does this letter conceal, answering its final question?

Your solving time: _____

▪ Line Fit ▪

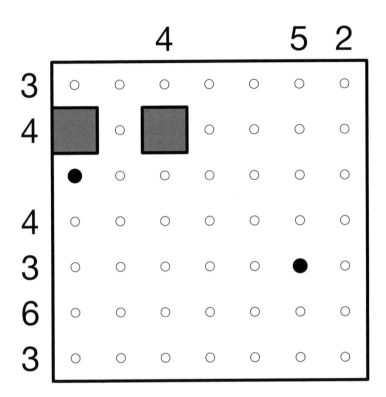

Instructions

Draw a path that joins one black dot to the other, traveling via the white dots using only horizontal and vertical lines.

- The path can't cross any shaded squares, and it can't use any dot more than once.
- Numbers outside the grid reveal the total number of dots visited by the path in their corresponding row or column.

Your solving time: _____   71

■ No Four in a Row ■

			X		X	X	
O	X	X		X	X	X	
		X				O	O
		O	O		O		
							O
		X	X			O	O
X	O			O		X	O
X		X		O		O	

Instructions

Place either an "X" or an "O" into each empty square so that no lines of four or more "X"s or "O"s are formed in any direction, including diagonally.

Your solving time: _____

■ A Trick of Logic ■

Three keen amateur magicians, Sylvester, Cassandra, and Sid, had met up to test their tricks on one another. Once they had all assembled, Sylvester showed them an opaque silk bag, but did not show what was inside.

"In this bag are a ball, a toy block, a die, and a pen. Each object is one of these six colors: red, yellow, blue, purple, green, or orange. I have written my name on one of these objects. Can you work out both the color and type of object I have written on?

"To help you, I will narrow down the range of colors for each object: the ball is yellow, blue, or orange; the toy block is purple or green; the die is red or blue; the pen is red, yellow, or purple."

Sylvester then told Cassandra what type of object had his name on it, but not its color. He next told Sid the color of the same object, but not what type of object it was.

At this point, Cassandra said to Sid, "I don't know what color the object with Sylvester's name is, but I am certain that you don't know what the object is."

Sid replied, "You're right, I didn't know before, but now I do."

Cassandra replied, "Well in that case, I know the color as well. This is logic, not a magic trick!"

Which object had Sylvester's name on, and what color was it?

▪ A Mug's Game ▪

Two friends, Giulia and Marie, lived in a building a hundred floors high. They owned some robust stoneware mugs, and Giulia told Marie that the person who sold them to her had claimed that they could be dropped from extreme heights without breaking.

There was a window in the stairwell on every floor that looked over a courtyard, which was empty, so the two friends decided to test this claim. They made a plan to drop the mugs from these windows on different floors in order to work out the minimum height of floors at which the mugs would break if dropped.

Giulia wanted to break no more than two of them in the name of science. All of the mugs were identical, and they assumed that, if a mug did not break, no damage would have been inflicted on it that would influence how likely it was to break in future.

They also assumed that if a mug broke when dropped from a particular floor, it would also break if dropped from a higher floor; and, if it did not break, then it would also not break if dropped from a lower floor. Neither of them was completely sure that the mug would not break if dropped from the first floor, or that it would definitely break if dropped from the top floor.

Assuming they used an optimal strategy, what is the maximum number of drops they would ever need in order to determine the lowest floor at which a mug will break? Remember that they only had two mugs with which they were able to test.

Your solving time: _____

▪ Train Tracks ▪

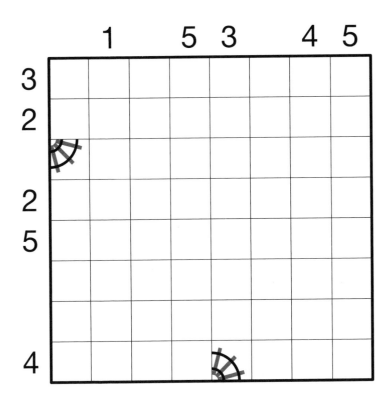

Instructions

Draw track pieces in some squares to complete a track that travels all the way from its entrance in the leftmost column to its exit in the bottom row.

- The track can't otherwise exit the grid, and nor can it cross itself.
- Numbers outside the grid reveal the number of track pieces in each row and column.
- Every track piece must either go straight or turn a right-angled corner.

Your solving time: _____

▪ Disco Dancing ▪

A group of forty-five lighting designers decided to throw a party, and to make the party more light-filled and fun, they decided to give each designer an LED light to carry around with them.

These lights were always one of pink, green, or orange, and were programmed to change color in some cases when lighting designers shook hands. If two designers with different colored lights shook hands, both of their lights would change into the third color—so if two designers with a pink and a green light respectively shook hands, both lights would turn orange. If designers with the same colored lights shook hands, nothing changed.

- Thirteen designers started with pink lights.
- Fifteen started with green lights.
- Seventeen started with orange lights.

Would it ever be possible for all of the designers to have the same color light at any point during the party?

Your solving time: _____

■ Four Winds ■

Instructions

Draw one or more horizontal or vertical lines emanating from each numbered square.

- Lines cannot cross numbered squares or enter the same square as another line.
- Each number indicates how many squares its lines travel into; the numbered squares themselves are not counted.
- All squares must be visited by a line.
- Each line can only connect to a single number.

Your solving time: _____

▪ A Dearth of Desserts ▪

The chairman of a philosophy club is hosting a potluck dinner party, where each of the guests is instructed to bring one dish. He phones around his guests, asking them to bring an appetizer, a main course, or a dessert.

Lots of the guests volunteer to bring appetizers or main courses, but the chairman finds himself very short on desserts. He calls up the final attendee on his list, determined to get her to bring a dessert. However, the attendee, eager to demonstrate her reasoning skills to the chairman, decides to set her host a challenge before accepting.

"Perhaps I will bring a dish," she says, "but it will be the type of dish that I want to bring. The only way you will persuade me to bring a dessert is to make a statement that will force me to do so, according to my rules:

"If you make a true statement, I will bring you the dish of my choice.

"If you make a false statement, I will bring no dish at all."

What can the chairman say to his guest to ensure that she brings a dessert to his dinner party? He needs a statement that she cannot falsify while following her own rules, and which forces a dessert as her only option.

Your solving time: _____

■ Every Second Turn ■

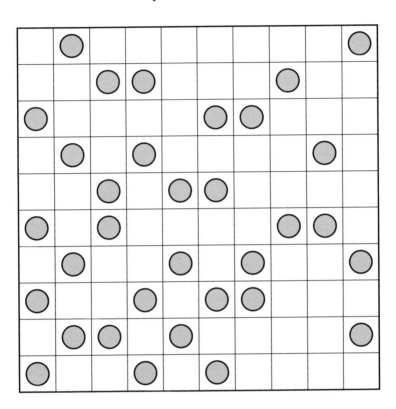

Instructions

Draw a loop that visits every square exactly once, consisting of horizontal and vertical lines between squares.

• Every second turn on the loop is indicated by a circle.

Your solving time: _____

■ Arrow Maze ■

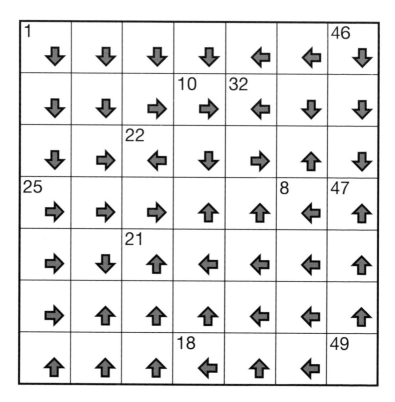

Instructions

Add numbers to the grid so that every square contains a
number, and each number from 1 to 49 appears exactly once.

• Every number must be in a square with an arrow that points
  in the precise direction of the next highest number.

Your solving time: _____

▪ Brotherly Competition ▪

Two brothers decide to have a running race on a hot summer's day. They mark out a track which measures 100 meters in length and agree to run from one end of the track to the other.

They race and the older brother wins, crossing the line at the exact moment that the younger brother crosses the 90-meter mark.

After their race, they decide to race back to their home, which is a 100 meters from where they are standing, agreeing that the last brother to reach home will give the other a prize.

The younger brother feels a little hard done by, and asks his older brother to start farther away from home than him, hoping that this will help him to win the race. The older brother agrees, and retreats back 10 meters, so that he is now 110 meters from home.

Assuming the brothers set off at the same time, and run at the same constant speeds they did in the first race, which brother will reach home first and receive the prize?

_____

_____

▪ **Early Retirement** ▪

A notice is sent to all of the employees working in a certain office. It contains the following message:

"As of next year, all employees will be entitled to retire at the age of fifty-five with full pension."

One woman in the office is particularly pleased with this news, saying, "Fantastic! That means I can retire next year!"

Her colleague at the next desk comments, "And you were only fifty-two the day before yesterday. That's lucky!"

Assuming they are both correct, how can this be true?

Your solving time: _____

■ Meadows ■

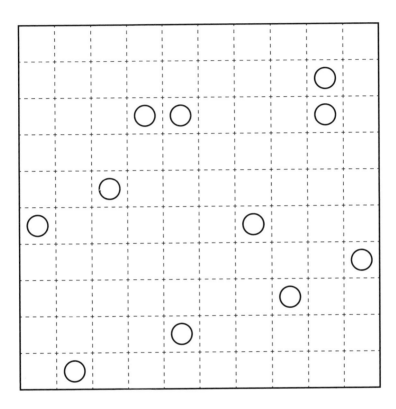

Instructions

Draw along the dashed lines to divide the grid into squares measuring 1×1 units or larger, with no unused areas left over.

• Every square must contain exactly one circle.

Your solving time: _____

▪ Bridges ▪

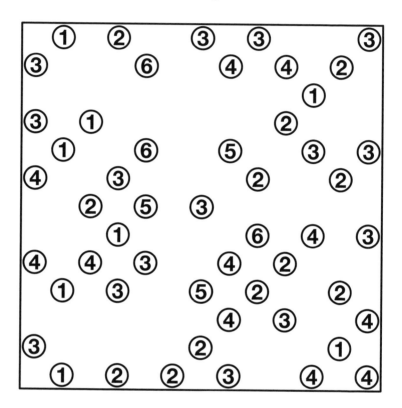

Instructions

Draw horizontal and vertical lines to represent bridges joining pairs of islands. Islands are indicated by circled numbers, where the number specifies the number of bridges that connect to that island.

- Any pair of islands may be joined by up to two bridges.
- Bridges may not cross either another bridge or an island.
- All islands must be joined together by the bridges, so you can travel to any island just by following the bridges.

Your solving time: _____

▪ A Shortage of Glasses ▪

The owner of the Anchor pub has recently employed three new members of staff to work behind the bar in the Mayflower, another pub that he also owns, located a short distance away. Each of the three new employees has recently commented that they are running short on wine glasses in the Mayflower, so he packages up fifteen new wine glasses, placing them into three boxes of different sizes, with five glasses placed into each box.

He asks one of the staff members at the Anchor to walk over to the Mayflower and deliver the glasses to the new employees, asking him to take care so that when he arrives all three boxes will all still contain five glasses.

On the way, however, the Anchor staff member bumps into someone who is running along the street, and drops one of the boxes. All of the glasses in the box are smashed, and he is forced to empty the box into a trash can.

How can he organize the glasses and boxes that he has left so that all three boxes still contain five glasses each? In this way he can fulfill his boss's requirement, even though he has lost five glasses on the way.

Your solving time: _____

▪ Tourist Truths ▪

A tourist visits an unusual town, which is accessible only by water. After spending a few days there, the tourist realizes that the town's inhabitants can be sorted into two categories: people who always tell the truth, and people who always lie.

The tourist decides to leave the town, and walks down to the jetty where he can get a boat to take him away. There is no timetable to indicate when the boats leave and arrive, but he sees a boatman who he knows is from the town waiting by the dock.

Knowing that the boatman is either always telling the truth or always lying, the tourist asks whether he can get a boat out of town this evening, or whether he will have to wait until the morning to travel.

The boatman replies, "If I am one of those who always tells the truth, then the boat will leave this evening."

Can the tourist leave town this evening? Assume a liar is someone who states the opposite of what is true.

Your solving time: _____

■ Multi Loops ■

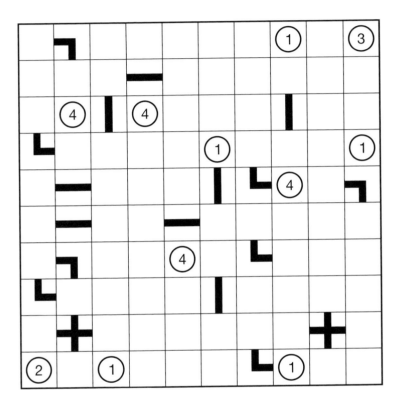

Instructions

Draw a set of loops that together pass through all squares, so at least one loop visits every square of the grid. In each square a loop may pass straight through, turn 90 degrees, or cross directly over another loop segment.

- Apart from in crossing squares, only one loop may enter any one square.
- Lines can never be drawn diagonally.
- Each loop must pass through at least one circle, and all circles with the same number must be part of the same loop and no other. Squares with given loop segments cannot be changed.

Your solving time: _____

▪ Minesweeper ▪

1	2		2		2		
				3		2	
2		1					1
	3		5		3	2	
2			5				
		3			2	2	
2			4		3		2
	3				3		2

Instructions

Place mines into some empty squares in the grid. Clues
in some squares show the number of mines in touching
squares—including diagonally.

• No more than one mine may be placed per square.

Your solving time: _____

▪ Grape Expectations ▪

Two mathematicians are having lunch. One mathematician removes twenty grapes from a bunch he is eating and places them onto the table in front of him.

He asks his colleague to arrange the grapes into five rows, each containing four grapes.

She does so, forming five horizontal lines, all parallel to one another, each with four grapes in it.

The first mathematician then takes away ten of the grapes, leaving ten still on the table.

He next asks his colleague to once again arrange the grapes so that they are in five rows, with exactly four grapes in each row.

How can it be done?

■ Family Matters ■

A woman draws out her family tree.

According to the tree she has three daughters, each of whom has two sisters and two brothers.

Two of her children each have two daughters of their own, while the remainder of her children have two sons each—and each of those sons has one sister.

How many grandchildren does the woman have?

Your solving time: _____

▪ Yin Yang ▪

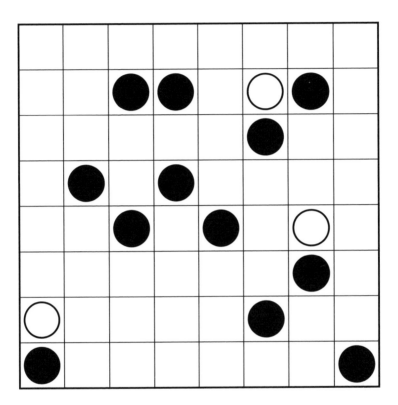

Instructions

Every empty square must have either a black or a white circle added to it. All circles of the same color must form a single continuous region, where you can travel from any circle of that color to any other of the same color while stepping only via circles of that color.

- Steps can only be horizontally or vertically between touching squares.
- There may not be any 2×2 areas of the same color.

Your solving time: _____   **91**

▪ Sock Selection ▪

A blind man is leaving for a four-day conference and is packing his bag in a hurry. His wardrobe contains only clothes that are black or white, which makes it easy to coordinate his outfits.

He comes to his sock drawer and realizes that none of his socks are paired up. He needs four matching pairs—one for each day of the conference. The drawer contains socks that are either black or white, with enough socks to form a dozen pairs of each type.

He begins taking socks out of the drawer, unable due to his blindness to see which color each sock is as he removes it from the drawer.

What is the smallest number of individual socks that he needs to take from the drawer in order to guarantee that he takes four matching pairs with him to the conference?

Your solving time: _____

▪ **Gaps** ▪

	1	1	2	1	1	1	1	1	2
5									
1									
5									
1									
7									
3									
3									
1									
1									

Instructions

Shade two squares in every row and column so that the number of unshaded squares between those two squares is equal to the number at the start of the corresponding row or column.

• Shaded squares do not touch, not even diagonally.

Your solving time: _____   93

▪ **Snake** ▪

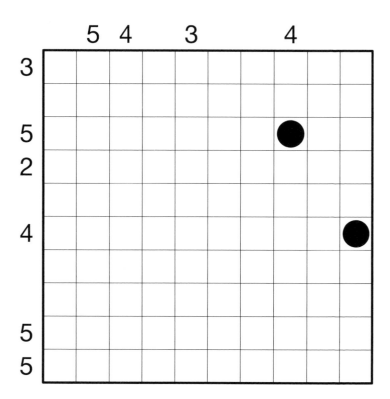

Instructions

Shade some squares to form a single snake that starts and ends at the squares marked with circles.

- A snake is a path of adjacent squares that does not branch or cross over itself.
- The snake does not touch itself—not even diagonally, except when turning a corner.
- Numbers outside the grid reveal the number of squares in their row or column that contain part of the snake.

Your solving time: _____

▪ Cattle Conundrum ▪

A farmer is on his way to market, where he intends to buy a cow. Cows cost two coins, so the farmer makes sure he has at least two coins in his money pouch.

The farmer knows that, on the way, he will encounter seven gates, each of which requires a toll to be paid before it will be opened.

The gatekeepers do not have fixed toll prices, but instead always demand that the payment is half the number of coins that a traveler has with them, rounding up if necessary to ensure a whole number of coins. As a token of kindness, however, the gatekeepers always give back one coin to the traveler after they have opened their gate.

The farmer thinks about the gatekeeper tolls as he prepares to leave for the market.

How many coins should he leave the house with, to ensure that he arrives at the market with exactly two coins left so that he can buy his cow? Assume that the tolls will all be free on his return, and that he wants to travel with as few coins as possible.

_____

_____

▪ **Bus Allotment** ▪

A gardener has two allotments, both of which are a bus ride away. Both allotments require equal care and attention to flourish and should be visited every other day.

The allotments are on two different sides of her town—one to the east, and one to the west. The gardener decides that, to visit the gardens with equal frequency over the course of a year, she will use the network of buses that travel between the east and west of the city.

She plans to walk to the bus terminal near her house in the middle of town at a random time each day and get on the next bus to leave after the time she arrives, regardless of whether it is going east or west. Only buses going in these two directions depart from the bus terminal, and each of the buses travel past one of her two allotments. The buses always leave on time from the bus terminal, and both the east and the west buses leave five times every hour, each departing at twelve-minute intervals.

It turns out, however, even if she always arrives at the bus terminal at a truly random time, that three quarters of all her trips will be to the west allotment, and only a quarter to the east allotment.

Why would this be?

Your solving time: _____

▪ **Lasers** ▪

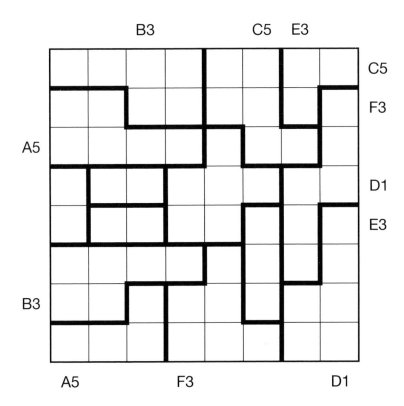

Instructions

Draw diagonal lines across certain squares to form mirrors, with exactly one mirror per bold-lined region.

- The mirrors must be placed so that a laser fired perpendicularly into the grid from each lettered clue would then exit the grid at the same letter elsewhere, having bounced off the exact number of mirrors indicated by the number next to the letter.

Your solving time: _____   **97**

▪ Mountain Maths ▪

A mountaineer stands at the top of a mountain and takes a series of photos before heading back down to the village below.

It takes him four hours to climb down the mountain, and the mountaineer leaves the top at noon, knowing that the distance to the bottom is six kilometers. On the way down, he hears the sound of some church bells giving the time as 3:00 p.m., and notices that he is two kilometers away from the bottom of the mountain. He reaches the bottom of the mountain at 4:00 p.m., only to discover—to his intense annoyance—that he has left his camera at the top of the mountain. He therefore decides to stay overnight before climbing to the summit again in the morning to retrieve his camera.

He sets off to climb the mountain at noon the following day and arrives at the summit at 4:00 p.m., having retraced his steps all the way to the top.

The ascent and descent both took exactly four hours, from noon to 4:00 p.m., on consecutive days.

What is the likelihood that the mountaineer, at some point in his journeys up or down the mountain, was in exactly the same location at exactly the same time on both days?

Your solving time: _____

▪ Dominoes ▪

0	3	1	5	0	2	2	0
4	6	6	5	2	3	3	3
5	2	2	1	4	6	1	5
1	6	5	6	1	6	4	2
3	3	1	0	3	2	4	6
6	1	4	0	0	2	4	0
4	1	3	0	4	5	5	5

Instructions

Draw solid lines to divide the grid to form a complete set of standard dominoes, with exactly one of each domino.

	0	1	2	3	4	5	6
0							
1							
2							
3							
4							
5							
6							

- A "0" represents a blank on a traditional domino.
- Use the check-off chart to help you keep track of which dominoes you've placed.

Your solving time: _____   99

▪ Shady Question ▪

Two artists are painting next to one another. One has a pot of blue paint, and the other has pot of yellow paint, and the two pots contain the same amount of paint. They decide they would both rather have green paint, although they don't much mind what shade of green.

Using a spoon, the artist with blue paint takes a glob from his pot, and puts it into the pot of yellow paint. He roughly mixes it in, and then takes an identically sized glob of the mixed paint and puts it back into his own pot. He mixes it up, and observes the results. They both now have the same amount of green-hued paint, although the shades are very different.

The artist who started with the yellow paint says, "My green paint is a much lighter shade than yours. There must be less blue paint in my pot than there is yellow paint in your pot."

Is she right about the proportions of paint?

Your solving time: _____

■ **Walls** ■

	5					5		
			8					
	2						5	
5				6		1		4
		2				1		
5		2		5				4
	3						6	
				6				
		2					3	

Instructions

Draw a horizontal or vertical line across the full width or height of the center of every white square.

- The total length of all lines touching each black square must be equal to the number printed on that cell.
- The length of a line is defined as the number of squares it covers.
- Some lines may be shared between black squares; other lines may not touch any black squares.

Your solving time: _____

▪ Loop Finder ▪

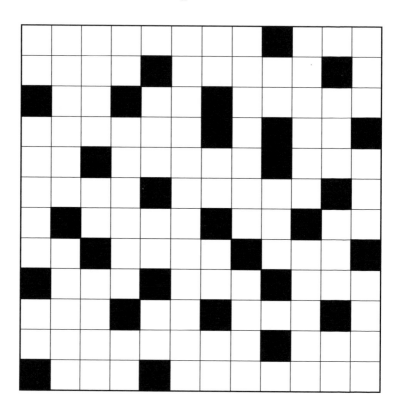

Instructions

Draw a single loop that visits every white square exactly once.

- The loop cannot touch or cross over either itself or a black square at any point.
- The loop consists only of horizontal and vertical line segments.

Your solving time: _____

■ Millinery Mix ■

A group of millinery models had become bored with the fashion show circuit, so at one show they asked the designer to come up with a game to keep them entertained. The designer agreed and explained the rules to them.

"You will all wear a hat of a single color. There will be a large number of different colors of hat being worn, but you will not be able to see your own as it will be put on your head by my assistant while you are blindfolded. The room where the fashion show will take place does not have any mirrors or reflective surfaces, so you will not be able to see your own hat during the show itself.

"You will all walk onto the stage at the same time and will at that point be able to look at the hats worn by the other models. The song on the sound system will change at intervals, and you may leave the stage whenever the song changes, but only if you are certain of the color of your own hat. I will be standing at the side of the stage and will ask you the color of your hat as you leave.

"One more thing: I promise that it will be possible for *all* of you to work out the color of your hat."

Assuming the stage is not empty, what is the minimum number of hats of any one color that will be left on the stage after the first song change, and models who know the color of their hats have already left? Assume that all the models approach the game using optimal logic and leave as soon as possible.

▪ Keeping Time ▪

Many years ago, a shopkeeper in a small town suddenly noticed that his clock had stopped. He had been busy completing an inventory in his stockroom and had lost track of time. He was particularly fastidious and always closed his shop at the same time every day, and this clock was his only way of knowing the time. After winding his stopped clock, he set out to find the current time.

There was no way for the shopkeeper to check the exact time using another clock, as there were none in the town's public spaces and he was too shy to ask the time of anyone else. However, he was friendly with the owner of a clock shop a couple of miles away, so he decided to walk over to ascertain the time from her.

He walked with an even pace to the clock shop and greeted the shopkeeper. After spending a while catching up with her over a cup of tea, he left to go back to his shop, making an effort to walk at the same speed as he had on his outward journey. As soon as he returned home, he set his clock to almost exactly the correct time.

How did the shopkeeper work out what time to set the clock to when he returned from his trip?

■ Entries and Exits ■

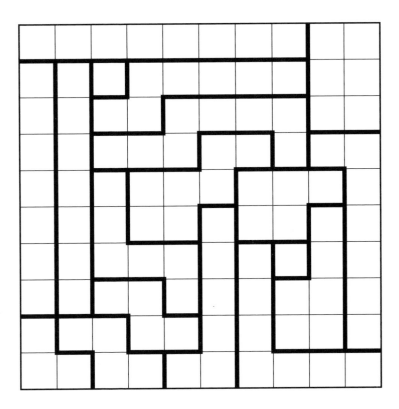

Instructions

Draw a loop that visits every square.

- The loop should only travel horizontally or vertically and cannot visit any square more than once.
- The loop can only enter and exit each bold-lined region once.

Your solving time: _____

▪ Area Division ▪

F	C	G	F	D	F	E	H
C	D	D	G	C	C	G	B
B	E	A	E	E	A	E	F
A	D	C	H	D	H	A	C
H	G	B	F	B	H	B	H
B	G	F	A	E	E	D	B
C	D	H	H	G	B	G	G
A	F	E	A	F	C	A	D

Instructions

Draw along some of the dashed lines to divide the grid into a set of areas, each containing one of every letter from A to H.

Your solving time: _____

▪ Bridge Dilemma ▪

A woman is walking home from the pet shop when she arrives at a very narrow bridge over a gorge. She is carrying three new pets with her: a dog, a cat, and a goldfish in a bowl of water.

The bridge is unstable, and the woman knows she can only carry one of the pets across with her at any one time. She picks up the dog, intending to take it over first, but then realizes that the cat will eat the fish if they are left alone together. She picks up the fish to take it over, and then realizes instead that the dog will chase the cat away if they're left alone together. She puts down the fish.

How can she get all three new pets across the river, without any of them being eaten or chased away at either end?

Your solving time: _____   **107**

▪ Picky Client ▪

An architect is building a house for a demanding client.

The client wants the house to be a perfect square, with two windows on each of the four walls. The client also wants all of the windows in the house to be facing south, to guarantee maximum sunshine.

The client also wants the exterior of the house to be landscaped so that if he walked a mile south from his front door, then a mile east, and then a mile north, he would still return to his front door.

Where should the client's house be built, and where should the front door be?

Your solving time: _____

■ Shape Link ■

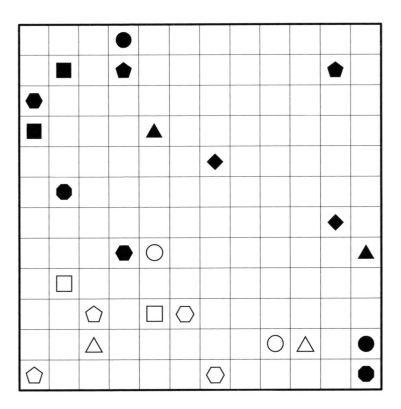

Instructions

Draw a series of separate paths, each connecting a pair of identical shapes.

- No more than one path can enter any square.
- Paths can only travel horizontally or vertically between squares.

Your solving time: _____   **109**

▪ The Marriage Proposal ▪

A man asks for a woman's hand in marriage. The next day, he receives this letter from the woman, who enjoys creating hidden puzzles:

> Yesterday you asked me to marry you, and I must thank you for the compliment. I should warn you that I cannot easily make up my mind and hope you will accept this response as my decision.
>
> This letter may seem to you the coyest way of responding—not to mention the most old-fashioned—but I am unconvinced that seeing you with my own eyes will help me to come to a conclusion. Indeed, the idea of seeing you in person does make me rather nervous. Are you sure you want to marry the shyest woman in the world?
>
> Please respond to me in the normal way—by post. I cannot bear long, painful goodbyes.

When the man finishes reading the letter, he knows the woman's decision has been made on balance, despite her evident indecision.

Is he engaged, or not?

Your solving time: _____

▪ **Line Fit** ▪

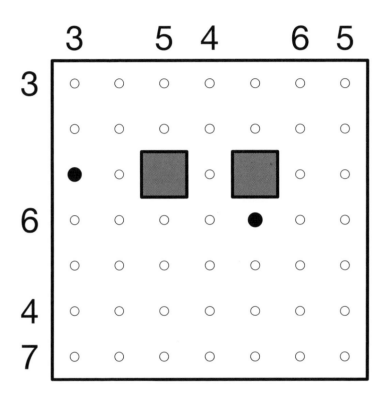

Instructions

Draw a path that joins one black dot to the other, traveling via the white dots using only horizontal and vertical lines.

- The path can't cross any shaded squares, and it can't use any dot more than once.
- Numbers outside the grid reveal the total number of dots visited by the path in their corresponding row or column.

Your solving time: _____   **111**

▪ Staring Contest ▪

Amy, Bob, Cat, Dom, and Eve are having a five-way staring contest, and anyone who blinks is eliminated.

- Dom blinks before Amy but wasn't the first to blink.
- Eve blinks before Cat does, but after Bob has already been eliminated.
- Eve blinks later than Amy.

Who blinked first, and who is the winner?

Your solving time: _____

▪ Skyscrapers ▪

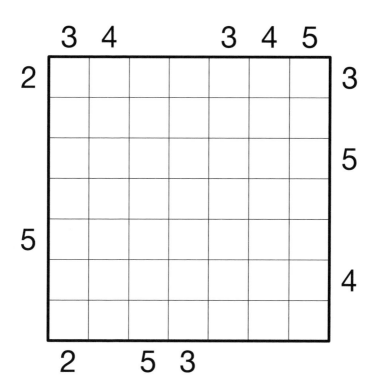

Instructions

Place a digit from 1 to 7 into every square, so that no digit repeats in any row or column inside the grid.

- Each clue number outside the grid gives the number of digits that are "visible" from that point, looking along that clue's row or column. A digit is visible unless there is a higher digit preceding it, reading from the clue along the row or column. E.g., in "2143576" the 2, 4, 5, and 7 are visible from the left, but 1 is obscured by the 2; 3 is obscured by the 4; and 6 is obscured by the 7—so its clue would be "4."

Your solving time: _____   **113**

▪ Shape Fit ▪

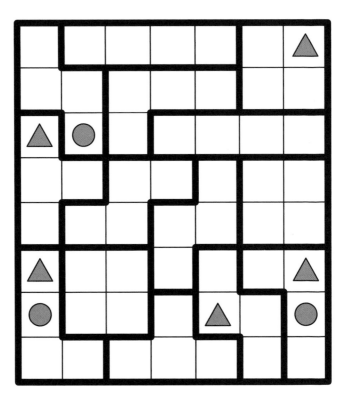

Instructions

Place circles and triangles into some squares so every bold-lined region contains exactly one circle and exactly one triangle. Two identical shapes cannot be in touching grid squares—not even diagonally.

Your solving time: _____

▪ Seven Secrets ▪

The following message arrives:

Sorry I've been out of touch—I've stopped picking up the phone, seeing as all I get is cold calls. I never thought I'd be a local celeb, as I like to keep a low profile, but I'm suddenly popular. Everyone is trying to get hold of my secret blend of seven herbs/spices, and they're using stealthy means.

The chronic love some people have for my blend is bizarre, but I'm entrusting the secret to you. Don't discard a momentous opportunity like this and, more importantly, don't tell a soul!

I'm in town next weekend, so I can tell you in person then, but look hard enough and you'll find all the ingredients in this note anyway.

It's tricky, though, and I'll be impressed if you can find all seven!

Can you?

_____

_____

Your solving time: _____

■ Sweet Rhubarb ■

A gardener gathers up rhubarb from her allotment, intending to make a large crumble.

She collects one kilogram of rhubarb stalks for her crumble and, while she gathers it, she remembers that a nutritionist friend of hers had once told her that rhubarb has a very high water content.

She decides to leave the bunch of rhubarb out in the sun for a day, so the sun would dry it out, thinking that rhubarb that contained less water would make a sweeter crumble.

If the one kilogram of rhubarb started out with 99 percent water content and dropped to 98 percent water content by the next day, what would the new weight of the rhubarb be?

Your solving time: _____

▪ **Fences** ▪

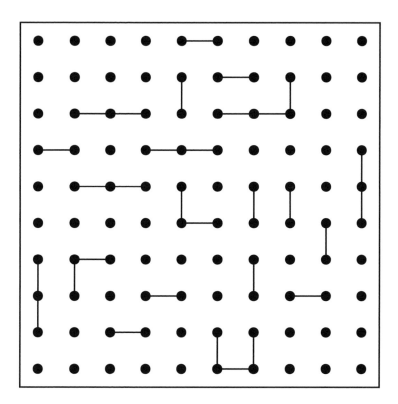

Instructions

Join all of the dots to form a single loop.

- The loop does not cross over or touch itself at any point.
- The loop can only consist of horizontal and vertical lines between dots.

Your solving time: _____

■ Triplet Takedown ■

A woman has committed a crime.

The suspects are narrowed down to three identical triplets—Sam, Sue, and Sal—who do not all tell the truth. In fact, one of them always lies, one of them always tells the truth, and one of them sometimes lies and sometimes tells the truth.

When interviewed, the women say the following:

• "I am the one who always lies," says Sam.
• "I am not the one who sometimes lies," says Sue.
• "I sometimes tell the truth," says Sal.

The investigators know that the perpetrator is the one who always lies. Which sister committed the crime?

Your solving time: _____

■ Easy as A, B, C, D ■

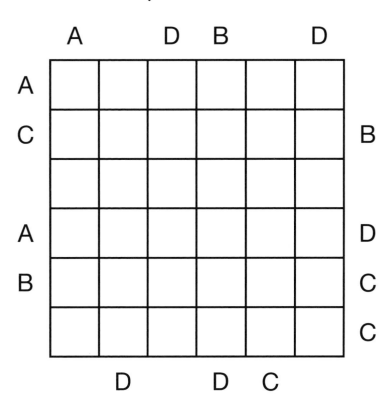

Instructions

Place A, B, C, and D once each into every row and column within the grid. This means that there will be one empty square in every row and column.

- Each letter given outside the grid must match the closest letter to it in within the same row/column.
- Letters may not share squares.

Your solving time: _____   **119**

▪ **Binary Puzzle** ▪

						1	
			0				
0		0		1			0
0			1			1	
	1				1		
						1	
		0		0			0
1	1			0	1		

Instructions

Place a 0 or 1 in every empty square so that there is an equal number of each digit in every row and column.

- Reading along a row or column, there may be no more than two of the same digit in succession.

Your solving time: _____

▪ Coin Conundrum ▪

A couple flip a coin every night to decide who washes the dishes after dinner. For several months, they do an equal amount of washing up, and both are happy.

After a while, one of the pair realizes that they have recently been losing the coin toss far more frequently than the other and as a result are having to do a lot more washing up. They inspect the coin and see that, in fact, the coin has been weighted so that it lands on one side more often than the other. It's a deliberate attempt to avoid doing the dishes.

They confront their partner, who confesses to tampering with the coin, and agrees that they should go back to the old system, with a fair coin.

But they can, in fact, still have a fair contest while flipping the unfair coin.

How can they use the unfair coin to produce the same results as flipping a fair coin, giving them both an even chance of avoiding doing the dishes?

Your solving time: _____   **121**

▪ The Three Jars ▪

Two chefs work in a kitchen together. It's a quiet day, and orders are slow, so one chef decides to play a prank on the other.

The kitchen contains several identical jars with different ingredients inside. The salt and sugar jars are labeled "salt" and "sugar" respectively. The mischievous chef takes off these labels and throws them away before finding a third jar, which is empty but otherwise identical to the now unlabeled jars. He pours an equal amount of salt and sugar into it, but does not stir the mixture. He finds three new labels, writes "sugar" on one, "salt" on another, and "blend" on the last. He puts one label on each jar, making sure they are all incorrect, and then turns to his unwitting colleague:

"These three jars are a riddle for you. None of the labels matches the content of its jar."

He points to an unfinished dessert next to him and continues:

"This crème brûlée is going out to the ambassador and needs sugar on top. You can only taste the contents of one of these three jars, and then you must decide which jar contains sugar, take a spoonful, and put it on the dessert. You'd better get this right or you'll be fired!"

The second chef needs to choose one jar to help her make her choice. Which of the three mislabeled jars should she taste the contents of?

Your solving time: _____

▪ Inbetweener ▪

			4	6		5	
	2			6			
	1		6		3		
	3				1		5
1	3		5		12		7
	5				6		6
4		3	7	8		8	
		6					5

Instructions

Draw along the grid lines to divide all of the grid into regions, so every region contains two numbers.

- Each region must contain a number of grid squares that is strictly between the value of the two numbers. So if the numbers are 5 and 12 then the region must contain between six and eleven squares.

Your solving time: _____

▪ Clouds ▪

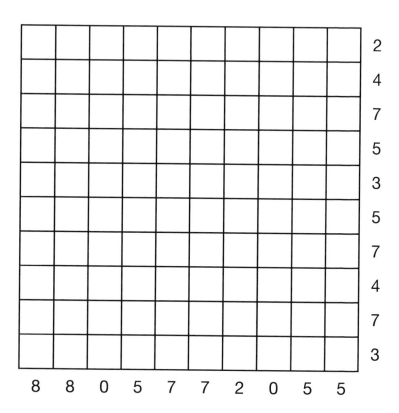

Instructions

Shade rectangular groups of grid cells, such that each group is at least two cells wide and at least two cells tall.

- Rectangular groups of cells cannot touch, not even diagonally.
- Given number clues specify the number of shaded cells in each row and column.

Your solving time: _____

▪ Spy Sending ▪

Two spies are sending confidential documents to one another. To ensure that their documents are not intercepted and stolen, they always send their dossiers in a sealed box, which can be locked with a padlock. Each spy owns one padlock and a single key—which is for their own padlock. For security, there are no copies of the keys, and each spy must keep their own key on their person at all times. It costs five dollars for each spy to send the sealed box to the other.

One spy needs to send a dossier to the other, using the sealed box.

How much will it cost to send them the dossier, given that it must never be sent in an unlocked box, and the receiving spy needs to open it to access the dossier?

Your solving time: _____

▪ **Jewelry Journal** ▪

A strange message arrives:

Before you run off and report this to the bank, let me just explain myself.

After I spent a year in Grandma's house, I noticed things were going missing:

That pink scarf.

Her favorite cacti; a range of books.

Most importantly, some top-end antique jewelry.

So I took what jewelry was left and smuggled it out, wrapped it in her old turban, gleaning that it must have been a family member stealing her things.

This doesn't count as a theft or crime—I'm sure of it.

I've hidden the last eight pieces of jewelry in the clock etched with Grandma's initials, at my place—but you can also find one per sentence.

What are the eight items of jewelry?

Your solving time: _____

▪ Loop the Loop ▪

```
3 . 1 . 2 . 2 . 0 . 0 .     . 3 . 2 .     .
3 .   0 .   2 .         1   2         .
2 .           2   3       0 . 3
1   0     0     1       1   1   3
1     1   1     2   1       0   3
2 . 3     3 . 1 .   1   3       3
2 . 2 . 2     1 .   3       0   2 .
2 . 3 .   3   3           .     1 .
  1   0     .   3       3     1
    0   0       3   2   2   1   2   3
```

Instructions
Connect some of the dots to create a single loop, so that each digit has the specified number of adjacent line segments.

- Dots can only be joined by horizontal or vertical lines.
- Each dot can be used no more than once.

▪ Line Sweeper ▪

		5						
				8	7			
	7							
				8				
		8						
				7				4
								3
		5						
				5				

Instructions

Draw a single loop that passes through some of the empty squares, using horizontal and vertical lines.

- The loop cannot re-enter any square.
- The loop must pass through the given number of touching squares next to each number clue, including diagonally touching squares.

Your solving time: _____

■ Green or Blue? ■

Frederika had been shopping and brought a box of chocolates and a stack of three new colorful notebooks back to her office.

The notebooks had covers with flat, unbroken colors. In fact, one of the books was green on both the front and the back, another was blue on both the front and the back, and the final book was green on one side and blue on the other. All of the notebooks had a black spine, so when lying flat it was impossible to see what color the side facing down was or to know if you were looking at the front or back of the book.

On the first page of the blue notebook she wrote "Admin"; on the first page of the green notebook she wrote "Meetings"; and on the first page of the blue-and-green notebook she wrote "Ideas." Meanwhile, her colleagues were eyeing up the chocolates, so she proposed a bet. She hid the notebooks and chose one at random, placing it flat on her desk. No one knew the color of the other side of the notebook, but the side facing up was green.

"The notebook I have placed on my desk can't be blue on both sides, as the side we can all see is green, meaning that the reverse side has to be either green or blue. This means that it is a fifty-fifty chance that it is either the notebook with 'Ideas' written on the first page, or the notebook with 'Meetings' written on the first page. So I will bet you, for ten chocolates, that the reverse, hidden side of this notebook is green."

Is this a fair bet, i.e. one with an even chance of either result?

▪ The Fifteenth Block ▪

A particularly picky customer was due at a cheese shop in the afternoon to pick up fifteen blocks of cheddar for a party. He required all fifteen blocks to be exactly the same weight.

The shop owner weighed and wrapped fourteen blocks of cheddar, ensuring they were all exactly the same weight using his electric scales. By the fifteenth block he had run out of cheddar, and so the last block weighed slightly less, but since it was visually indistinguishable from the rest he wrapped it anyway.

The shop owner went out for his lunch, leaving his assistant to run the shop alone. The assistant knew that the picky customer would be sure to notice as soon when he got home that one of the blocks of cheese was lighter than the rest, so decided to put aside the lighter block of cheese so he could ask the customer if he wanted it or not when he arrived. Unfortunately, the block was indeed visually indistinguishable, and the electric scales had been locked away by the owner. The only way he could determine the relative weight of the different blocks of cheese was using a pair of old-fashioned balancing scales.

The assistant needed to weigh the cheese quickly, before the customer arrived, to determine which was the odd one out.

How could the shop assistant determine which of the fifteen blocks of cheese was the light one, using a maximum of three comparisons on the balancing scales?

Your solving time: _____

▪ **Pipeline** ▪

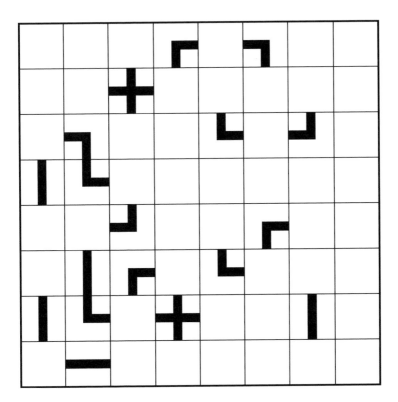

Instructions

Draw either a straight line, a corner, or a crossing segment in each empty square in order to form a single loop that visits every square.

- The loop may only travel horizontally or vertically between square centers.
- Some parts are given, and cannot be changed.

Your solving time: _____   **131**

▪ Hints ▪

Page 7

Ruby's sister has the pearl necklace, and we know that Ruby cannot have the ruby necklace, so what type of pendant must Ruby's necklace contain?

Page 9

In the third bullet we learn that Ant does not take the raft, and from the second bullet we also know that he doesn't use the kayak. So he must be in the canoe.

Page 10

The first key deduction is to decide when the man is known to be late. It's tempting to think this is at eight minutes past the hour, but it's actually at one minute past the hour.

Page 12

She is aiming to knit thirty hats but has created only half of them. Her original target was Christmas Eve, and she has done half as much work in the amount of time available.

Page 15

In the worst case, any set of thirteen jelly beans will all be different flavors. This means that, if she buys three sets of thirteen, she may still not have sufficient jelly beans.

Page 16

In the best case, all but one of the prisoners can be guaranteed to be released, and it's a fifty-fifty chance for the remaining prisoner. How can this be achieved?

▪ Hints ▪

Page 19

The new total of $29 is misleading. How exactly has this been calculated, and does that make sense? And is it definitely the case that it should have been $30 in any case?

Page 24

It's tempting to send over a fast and slow walker in each pair, for quick return of the umbrella, but is this really the best strategy?

Page 20

Start by working out which matches Gawain played, and then work out which matches Lancelot played. Did Gawain win any of his matches?

Page 26

There is only one day of the month where the situation described could arise. In what situation could the final piece of information disambiguate from the outstanding possibilities?

Page 23

Oli gets to shoot first, so who should he aim at? If he hits Jen, he is certain to be eliminated on the next shot. But if he hits Laila, he is still likely to be eliminated. Is there another option?

Page 29

Your brother is correct that you would need to break and reseal eight loops to join the existing chains end to end. But is there another way to do this?

▪ Hints ▪

Page 31

Each tap changes the state of three people. Note also that after three changes a person will have stood, sat, and then stood again. The solution involves tying these two "threes" together.

Page 37

There are only two possible "moves" if you do not know how much the stand has been rotated: either you choose adjacent ramekins or diagonally opposite ramekins.

Page 32

It helps to simplify the puzzle by splitting it into two scenarios: whether the assistant starts behind an even, or an odd, door. Consider the even scenario first.

Page 38

Olivia needs to make sure that Remi has exactly eleven lawns remaining to be mowed on the penultimate day, so no matter how many she chooses Olivia can still win.

Page 35

Simplify the situation by imagining that there were only two students. What would happen if they both had "apple" on their paper? Next, consider the situation with three students.

Page 41

Hint 1: Think about what most dice faces actually look like.

Hint 2: The diamond is set in the center, and the emerald totals are calculated from counting dice with a center spot.

■ Hints ■

Page 42

The text message is not quite so hurriedly written as it appears. Hidden within are several occasions of the words "up" and "down." Count how many there are of each word.

Page 48

The best you can be certain to do in general is to halve the remaining possibilities after each guess, so how would you do this as efficiently as possible?

Page 45

Consider how much soup will remain in the tureen after pouring as much of its content as will fit into the bowl. What if you now empty the bowl and pour the tureen's contents into it?

Page 50

Is the farmer's method relevant? What does the puzzle tell you about the relative likelihood of male and female calves? Does his method change the underlying probability?

Page 47

It's important to note that you can light both ends of an incense stick, which would halve its burn time. You can also light more than one stick at a time.

Page 53

The sequence is a logical one, based on parsing each number correctly. It does not require any existing general or mathematical knowledge.

▪ Hints ▪

Page 54

It's mostly a case of experimenting. Remember that there are 50-pence, 20-pence, 10-pence, 5-pence, 2-pence, and 1-penny coins in circulation. Start by deciding if he is likely to have any 1-penny coins.

Page 57

You can use school mathematics to solve this. Remember that to calculate the radius of a circle you simply divide the circumference of the circle by two times pi (and pi = 3.1415).

Page 59

Eventually, Gwen wants to leave Oli with two rows with one apple each, or two rows where both have an even number of apples. How can she get to this situation?

Page 60

If the answer isn't immediately obvious, it's probably best to work this out by experimenting with various values. Could she have one child? Two children? Three children? And so on.

Page 63

The bus she's on is traveling towards the buses coming the other way, so the overall effect is that an oncoming bus comes towards her twice as fast as if she were stationary.

Page 65

Split the task into two parts: first of all work out how many coats were transferred from the first rack to the second, then work out how many need to be transferred back.

▪ Hints ▪

Page 66

You can solve this as a set of simultaneous equations, by substituting equivalences from one statement into the equivalence in a different statement.

Page 73

Cassandra is certain Sid doesn't know immediately, which provides key information. Sid also doesn't immediately know the answer, which further eliminates options.

Page 69

It's a system that the children would know and use on a regular basis and doesn't require any specialist knowledge to solve.

Page 74

If you only had one mug you would have to start at the bottom floor and work your way up, for a maximum of a hundred drops. But you can do much better once you have two mugs.

Page 70

The final sentence of the first paragraph refers to a "radio code," and indeed that's how the message has been encrypted. Each paragraph encodes a single word.

Page 76

For all of the lights to be a single color, there would have to be zero lights of the other two colors. Consider how the difference between the totals changes on each handshake.

▪ Hints ▪

Page 78

There is something you can say about the other two dishes, and not the dessert, to force her hand, so long as the statement cannot be false without her breaking her rules.

Page 85

The math of the situation is seemingly impossible, since there are now only ten glasses, so what else can they do to fulfill the literal requirements of the owner?

Page 81

At what point will the two brothers draw level in the second race? From that point, what will happen next? Which of the two brothers runs faster?

Page 86

If the boatman is telling the truth, the situation is simple. But what if they are a liar? The condition is falsified, but remember that they are also lying.

Page 82

What day of the year must it be today, and on what day of the year must the woman's birthday be? You can work out both of these, which gives you a hint as to how this can be true.

Page 89

Clearly the rows cannot be parallel horizontal rows, since there are now insufficient grapes for this to be possible. The rows must cross one another in some other way.

▪ **Hints** ▪

Page 90

Some care needs to be taken, since adding up the numbers can be misleading. Remember that a sister to a daughter is also a daughter, and similarly for brothers and sons.

Page 96

If the ten hourly departures, across the two buses, were evenly spaced, then she would visit each allotment the same number of times. So how must they instead be arranged?

Page 92

Try working through all of the possible combinations of socks that could result in having four matching pairs—and he would clearly need as a minimum at least eight separate socks.

Page 98

The title of the puzzle is somewhat misleading, since math is not required—or at least arithmetic is not needed, at any rate. There is a simpler observation you can make.

Page 95

He halves his number of coins at each step, and then adds one. Try working your way up from a low number of coins to find the minimum he requires.

Page 100

If the same total amount of paint is transferred one way as the other, then both pots have the same amount of paint. How is the ratio of the two colors defined?

▪ Hints ▪

Page 103

Can there ever be just one of a particular color of hat? And then consider what would happen if there were just two of a particular color of hat.

Page 104

The shopkeeper needs to remember the time on his incorrect clock when he first leaves his shop. This lets him calculate the total elapsed time on his trip. What then?

Page 107

The key observation is that the cat cannot be left alone with an animal. This means that on their first crossing they must take the cat with them. But then what?

Page 108

The client's expectations aren't very realistic. There is in fact only one place on earth where all of these conditions could be fulfilled. Where?

Page 110

How does the message start and end? In particular, what letters start and end the message, and what do they spell? Can you find any hidden "yeses" or "nos" in the message?

Page 112

It's helpful to write out the clues as a sequence of letters (A, B, C, D, E) in the order that the people must have blinked. You then have three sequences that can only fit together one way.

■ Hints ■

Page 115

There is one herb or spice concealed within every sentence. You must read letters across the joins between words to find the hidden ingredients.

Page 121

Each individual toss of the coin gives a weighted result, but what happens if they toss the coin twice? Can you say something about the likelihood of two successive tosses?

Page 116

Start by working out what the weight of the non-water part of the rhubarb was, when it weighed one kilogram. Then, after evaporation, what percentage of the rhubarb is this?

Page 122

They need to choose a jar where they can be sure what they're tasting, so they want to make sure they don't taste the blend because they may not be able to identify it reliably.

Page 118

Start by considering the first clue. If Sam always lied then this statement would be true, so there is an immediate contradiction. Then consider the second statement similarly.

Page 125

Neither spy has the other's key, and they can't post the keys, so what multistage process can be used to work around these restrictions and still let them access the dossier?

▪ **Hints** ▪

Page 126

As the message suggests, there is one item of jewelry hidden within each sentence. They can be all found across the joins between one or more words.

Page 129

It's important to note that there are a total of four sides on the two notebooks it could possibly be, and her colleagues don't know which way up the notebook is.

Page 130

The secret is to start by splitting the fifteen blocks into three groups of five, and then to balance one of those sets of five against a second set of five. Then what do you do next?

▪ **Solutions** ▪

Page 7

Pearl has the ruby necklace.

We know that Ruby cannot have the ruby necklace as they share a name. It is also known that Ruby has not been given the pearl necklace, as one of her sisters says in the conversation that she has been given it. This means that Ruby must be wearing the amber necklace, leaving only the ruby and pearl necklace to assign to their owners. Pearl cannot be wearing the pearl necklace, so she must be wearing the ruby necklace, leaving Amber with the pearl necklace.

Page 8

O	X	O	X	O	X	X	X
O	X	X	X	O	X	O	O
X	O	X	O	O	O	X	O
X	O	O	O	X	O	O	X
X	X	O	X	X	X	O	X
O	X	X	X	O	X	X	X
X	O	O	O	X	O	O	O
O	X	X	O	X	X	O	O

Page 9

The owl crosses in a raft, with Cal.

We know from the last clue that Ant is not in the raft, and from the second clue that he is not in the kayak, so he must be in the canoe. Therefore, Cal is in the raft and Ben, as stated, is in the kayak. We also are told that the canoe must hold the dog, and the kayak does not have the owl so must have the cat. This leaves the owl to go in the raft.

The combinations are therefore as follows:

- Ant takes the dog in the canoe.
- Ben takes the cat in the kayak.
- Cal takes the owl in the raft.

▪ **Solutions** ▪

Page 10

There are three slices of pizza left.

The chef will eat one slice of pizza at 8:01 p.m., since the customer is at this point late, which he would not have been if a slice had been eaten at 8:00 p.m. or earlier. He will then eat a second slice at 8:09, a third at 8:17, a fourth at 8:25, and a fifth at 8:33, meaning that there are three slices of pizza left when the customer arrives a minute later.

Page 11

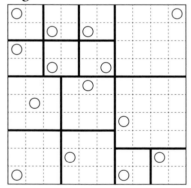

Page 12

The grandmother has her realization on Christmas Eve.

We know that she must start the knitting fifteen weeks before Christmas Eve, as she needs fifteen weeks to knit thirty hats at a rate of two hats a week. If she has only knitted one hat a week, and has fifteen hats, then fifteen weeks must have passed—and it must be Christmas Eve already.

■ **Solutions** ■

Page 13

6	1	3	2	1	3	0	4
6	2	5	5	5	3	0	6
5	2	2	1	6	4	0	6
0	3	6	1	5	2	5	0
4	0	4	0	6	1	3	1
5	3	4	4	1	3	3	4
2	5	2	0	6	4	2	1

Page 14

H	A	F	B	G	D	B	H
D	C	F	B	D	F	E	G
G	C	A	H	H	C	C	A
D	A	E	D	G	E	C	A
A	B	F	D	G	C	H	E
B	F	H	E	A	B	F	G
C	E	H	C	G	B	A	B
H	G	E	F	E	D	D	F

Page 15

The woman must spend forty cents for her forty jelly beans.

If she spends thirty-nine cents for up to thirty-nine jelly beans, then she might be unlucky since she could end up with three each of all thirteen flavors. If she then buys a fortieth bean it must then be the fourth of a flavor—so forty is the minimum number that guarantees four beans of the same flavor.

▪ Solutions ▪

Page 16

Yes. The best strategy guarantees that at least forty-nine of the prisoners escape, with a fifty-fifty chance that all fifty of them do.

Beforehand, they should agree a strategy whereby if the prisoner at the back of the line—who can see every other hat—can see an odd number of green hats he should say "green," whereas if he can see an even number of green hats he should say "red." He, of course, has a fifty-fifty chance of being correct by chance. The prisoner in front of him, however, can count the number of green hats he can see in front of *him*, and if it matches the odd/even announcement of the prisoner behind him he can be certain that he must have a *red* hat on since if he had a green hat on then odd would have become even, and vice versa. He announces his correct hat color, and all the other prisoners then update their mental expectation of whether to see an even or odd number of green hats—i.e. if he says "red" they do not change it, while if he says "green" then they alternate between odd and even.

As they then work down the line, in the certainty that all the people behind them are correctly calling their hat color (apart from the first prisoner, who may have been incorrect), they can continue to update their expectations and then compare them against the number of hats in front of them. Every remaining prisoner can therefore announce the correct hat color.

Page 17

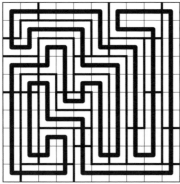

■ **Solutions** ■

Page 18

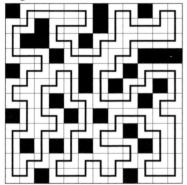

Page 19

The total of $29 is misleading. In fact, the party have now paid $27, which covers the $25 dinner and a $2 tip. The $2 tip is not *additional* to the $27, so the total of $29 never arises. The fact that this false total of $29 is $1 short of the original $30 is also irrelevant.

Page 20

Percival and Gawain, with the victory going to Percival.

Every player must play at least every other game, so for Gawain to joust in seven matches he must have jousted in every other match of the fifteen, starting at match two, and lost all of them. Because he did not take part in the other matches, there must have been eight matches between Lancelot and Percival. We also know Lancelot took part in the first nine matches, and then also must have taken part in matches eleven, thirteen, and fifteen, which Gawain was not a part of, to give the total of twelve matches. This means match fourteen must have been between Gawain and Percival, and we already know that Gawain lost all his matches.

■ **Solutions** ■

Page 21

Page 22

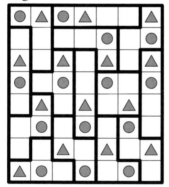

Page 23

The best strategy would be for Oli to deliberately miss both Jen and Laila until one of them is eliminated.

This requires an assumption that Jen and Laila would both see each other as the greatest threat and attempt to eliminate each other first, as they are both more accurate shots than Oli. Oli will therefore end up in a two-person competition with either Jen or Laila, and in either case he will have the first shot, giving him a slightly better than one in three chance of winning the trip (since his chance is one in three if aiming at Laila, or slightly better than that if aiming at Jen since she might miss and give him more than

▪ **Solutions** ▪

one shot)—at this point there will only be two shooters left and he will have the first shot, giving him the best chance of winning. Conversely, if he fires from the off and eliminates someone immediately, he will immediately have at best a one in six chance of winning (i.e., the two-in-three person missing him and he then hitting them); and clearly if he fires and hits the two-in-three person first then the certain shot would hit him and he would lose.

Page 24

First, Marcel should walk to the platform with Dani, which will take two minutes. Marcel then returns to the others, taking one minute. He passes the umbrella to Lola and Zara, who cross together, taking ten minutes. Dani takes the umbrella from them and crosses back over, taking two minutes. Dani and Marcel then cross the bridge together once again, taking two minutes. These journeys add up to seventeen minutes in total. Or, as an alternative solution, Dani could return after the first crossing, taking two minutes, with Marcel crossing back over in the fourth crossing, taking one minute. This would also lead to a total journey time of seventeen minutes.

Page 25

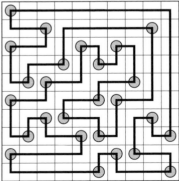

▪ Solutions ▪

Page 26

The children are aged three, three, and eight.

The second professor knows that the product of the ages is seventy-two, and also what the date is. But, because the second professor was still puzzled at this point, it means that the date must be such that there was more than one possibility for the combination of the total and the product. Looking at the possible combinations of ages that multiply to seventy-two, the only possible day of the month that would have this confusion is the fourteenth, since both 2 + 6 + 6 = 14 and also 3 + 3 + 8 = 14, noting that 2 x 6 x 6 = 72 and 3 x 3 x 8 = 72.

We also know that the final statement removes the ambiguity, so it must be that the reference to an "eldest child" resolves the ambiguity, eliminating the option where the two oldest children are both aged six—and so the second professor can finally deduce that the ages are three, three, and eight. Of course, it is not impossible that someone could refer to the older of two twins as "the eldest," but then the first professor would not be able to claim that his final fact gave a definitive answer—so we can dismiss this option.

Page 27

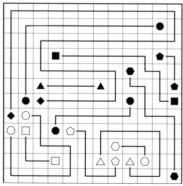

■ **Solutions** ■

Page 28

1	21	35	24	23	45	22
⬇	➡	⬇	⬇	⬅	⬇	⬅
2	20	19	3	18	47	8
➡	⬆	⬅	⬇	⬅	⬇	⬇
38	37	36	40	39	42	41
➡	⬅	⬅	➡	⬇	⬇	⬅
12	30	13	11	17	43	10
➡	⬇	⬇	⬅	⬆	⬇	⬅
32	31	34	4	33	46	9
➡	⬅	⬆	⬇	⬅	⬆	⬆
27	29	6	5	28	44	7
➡	⬆	➡	⬅	⬅	⬆	⬆
26	15	14	25	16	48	49
⬆	➡	⬅	⬅	⬆	➡	

Page 29

Your sister is correct—only seven loops need to be broken.

Following your brother's plan, you could break one of the end loops in each short chain and connect them together, meaning eight loops would need to be broken and resealed. However, you could also separate all seven loops in just one chain, giving you seven loops with which to connect the remaining seven short chains.

Page 30

1	0	1	0	0	1	1	0
0	0	1	0	1	1	0	1
0	1	0	1	0	0	1	1
1	0	0	1	1	0	1	0
0	1	1	0	1	1	0	0
0	0	1	1	0	0	1	1
1	1	0	1	0	1	0	0
1	1	0	0	1	0	0	1

▪ **Solutions** ▪

Page 31

Seven taps.

Simply tap on each person exactly once, in any order. This works because, after each tap, three people will change state between standing and sitting, or vice versa. By tapping on each person once, *every* person in the circle will therefore change state three times. This means every person will have stood, sat, and then stood again—and so all seven of them will be standing.

Page 32

Six. Guess the doors in the following order: 2, 3, 4, 2, 3, and then finally 4.

If the assistant starts behind an even-numbered door, they will be caught in one, two, or three guesses:

- If they are behind 2, they are caught in one guess.
- If they are behind 4, they will either move to 3 and be caught in two guesses, or to 5 and then back to 4 and be caught in three guesses.

If they start behind an odd-numbered door, then after the three guesses above they must now be behind an even-numbered door (since every time they move left or right they change between an odd and an even door), and so repeating the same sequence will find them exactly as described above. In the worst-case scenario it therefore takes six guesses to locate them.

▪ **Solutions** ▪

Page 33

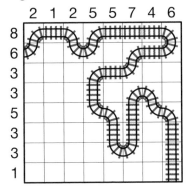

Page 34

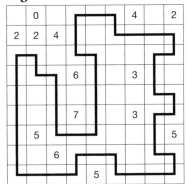

Page 35

Through inductive logic. Imagine if there were only two students. In such a case they would each look at each other's paper and see that the other person had "apple" written on it, but they wouldn't know if their own paper did. However, at the end of the first lesson they would see that the other student didn't come up to the lecturer, so they would know that their own piece of paper must have "apple" on it or otherwise the other student would have claimed a prize. They can therefore stand up at the next lesson to claim it.

Now consider if there are three students. Suppose you are one of these students. You know that if your paper did not say "apple"

▪ **Solutions** ▪

that the other two students would act in the same way as if there were only two students, as above, and one would come up to claim a prize after the second lecture. But when neither of them do, you therefore conclude this is not the situation and so you know that your paper must say "apple" on it. And so on and so on—as you add students, so you add lectures that must be attended to be sure of what's written on your own piece of paper.

Page 36

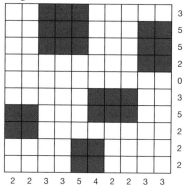

Page 37

Broadly speaking, at each turn the customer can turn either two adjacent ramekins or two that are diagonally opposite to one another. You can use this observation to come up with a technique that is guaranteed to succeed within five attempts:

• For the first turn, they should choose two ramekins diagonally across from each other and ensure they are both facing up. This will result either in a win or a second turn.

• For the second turn, they should choose two ramekins next to one another. At least one will be facing up following the first

▪ **Solutions** ▪

turn. If the other one is facing down, they should turn it over so both are facing up. This will result either in a win or three upturned ramekins.

- For the third turn, they should choose diagonally opposite ramekins again. If one is facing down, they should turn it over, which would result in a win. If both are the right way up, however, they should turn one of them over to create a situation where there are two adjacent ramekins the right way up and two adjacent ramekins the wrong way up.

- For the fourth turn, choose two ramekins that are next to each other and turn them both over regardless of which way up they are. You will either win or create a situation where two diagonally opposite ramekins are facing down.

- For the fifth turn, choose two diagonally opposite ramekins and reverse them so that all ramekins are the same way up, either facing up or down.

Page 38

Olivia would need to go first. She can come up with a winning plan by working backwards from the final lawn. Crucially, she needs to make sure that Remi is never left with ten or fewer lawns to mow, as he would be able to win. In fact, he must be left with eleven lawns in his final turn—any more, and he could guarantee the win for himself by simply leaving eleven for Olivia instead.

She should mow six lawns on the first day since this will leave forty-four to mow, which is a multiple of eleven, so she can guarantee that Remi will be left with eleven lawns at the end by making sure that their combined total for each subsequent pair of

▪ **Solutions** ▪

turns between them adds up to eleven. For example, if Remi mows four lawns after the first six, then Olivia can mow seven lawns, taking the number left to mow to thirty-three. She can then repeat the process, varying the number of lawns she mows to make sure Remi always starts on a multiple of eleven, until he has eleven lawns left to mow. At that point, he has to mow between one and ten lawns—and either way Olivia can win on the next day.

Page 39

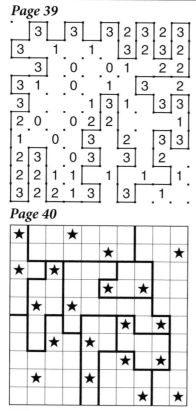

Page 40

▪ **Solutions** ▪

Page 41

The "diamond" in each instance is represented by the central dot present on some faces of a standard die, and the "emeralds" by the number of dots that surround this central dot on the relevant faces. The only faces on a standard die with a central dot *and* surrounding dots are 3 and 5. In each set of five rolls, the number of dots surrounding the central dot are totaled to give the number of emeralds—or, in other words, 2 is added for each roll of "3," and 4 is added for each roll of "5."

Page 42

The husband has been "up" more often than he has been "down." In the message, there are nine embedded "ups," in the following words: interru*p*ting, cu*p*board, stu*p*id, su*p*er, su*pp*ose, so*up*, su*pp*ort, *up*, and abru*pt*. By contrast there are only five embedded "downs": melt*down*, eider*down*, *down*stairs, *down*, and *down*. Overall, there are more ups than downs—and the first and last of these hidden words are also both "up."

Page 43

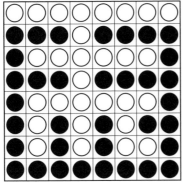

▪ **Solutions** ▪

Page 44

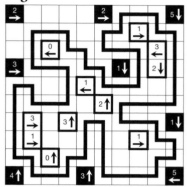

Page 45

The chef would need to start by filling the ten-liter tureen from the cooking vessel right up to its capacity, then pouring from the tureen into the six-liter bowl until the six-liter bowl was full. This would leave four liters in the ten-liter tureen.

After this, he would need to pour the soup in the six-liter bowl back into the cooking vessel and transfer the four liters of soup from the ten-liter tureen into the six-liter bowl. He would then need to refill the ten-liter tureen to capacity from the cooking vessel, and then pour the soup back out of the tureen into the six-liter bowl until the six-liter bowl was full—which would take two liters. This in turn would leave exactly eight liters of soup in the ten-liter tureen, and he could empty the six-liter bowl back into the cooking vessel ready for the waiters to eat.

Page 46

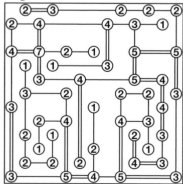

▪ **Solutions** ▪

Page 47

She would need to start by lighting both ends of one stick, and just one end of a second stick. The first stick would go out after twenty minutes, at which point the second stick would have twenty minutes of incense left to burn. At this point, she should light the unlit end of the second stick, causing the twenty minutes of burning time remaining on the second stick to be halved, giving an additional ten minutes on top of the twenty minutes given by the burning of the first stick. As a result, once the second stick is completely burned, she will know that thirty minutes has passed.

Page 48

Eleven guesses. The number can be guessed by halving the search space after each attempt. The second historian should always make their first guess 1000 (or 1001). Then if, for example, the year which the first historian had chosen was 1845, guessing 1000 would give the answer "that year is too early," eliminating the years between 1–1000. They can then guess in the middle of the remaining years, at 1500. By always halving the number of years left, it will always be possible to guess the correct year in eleven attempts or fewer. After one guess you will have up to 1000 years left; after two guesses up to 500; after three guesses up to 250; and so on with remaining totals of up to 125, 63, 31, 15, 7, 3, and then finally one number left either side—so you are guaranteed to get it on your eleventh guess.

Page 49

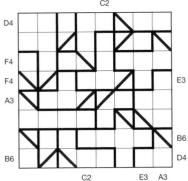

▪ **Solutions** ▪

Page 50

No—this plan could not be expected to work. For every birth there is an even likelihood of either a male or female calf, so the one-to-one ratio would on average be maintained even if the farmer used the described method.

Page 51

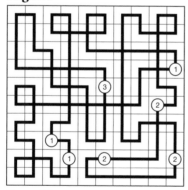

Page 52

			3				
2		2			5		3
	2			4		3	
1			4			5	
	3		5				1
			5			3	
		3		4			1
1	1	1	2		2		1

▪ **Solutions** ▪

Page 53

1113122115. The sequence is formed by reading out the digits from the previous number in order, grouping repeated digits of the same value by prefixing them by the number of times they appeared in sequence. The first entry is "5," so the following number is "one 5," written as "15." This has "one 1 one 5" so the following entry is "1115." This is "three 1s one 5" and so the next entry is "3115," and so on.

Page 54

The passer-by has one 50-pence coin, four 20-pence coins, one 5-pence coin, and four 2-pence coins. With these coins he is unable to provide complete change for a pound, 50 pence, 20 pence, 10 pence, or 5 pence.

Page 55

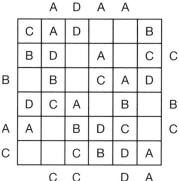

	A	D	A	A		
	C	A	D			B
	B	D		A		C	C
B		B		C	A	D
	D	C	A		B		B
A	A		B	D	C		C
C			C	B	D	A
		C	C		D	A

■ Solutions ■

Page 56

	3		3	4	6	3		
	7	5	6	4	3	1	2	5
3	1	2	7	6	4	3	5	3
2	5	1	2	7	6	4	3	4
	3	6	1	5	7	2	4	2
2	6	3	4	1	2	5	7	1
	4	7	3	2	5	6	1	
4	2	4	5	3	1	7	6	
			3	3				

Page 57

Yes, you could walk between the ribbon and the building, since the path would be around eighty centimeters wide—which is sufficiently broad for someone to walk along.

For the 2,500-meter-long circumference of the building, the radius is 397.9m (i.e. 2,500 divided by 2 × 3.1415, since the radius of a circle is equal to its circumference divided by two times pi). For a 2,505-meter-long circumference, the radius is 398.7m (i.e. 2,505 divided by 2 × 3.1415). The difference between 398.7m and 397.9m is 0.8m, i.e. eighty centimeters.

Page 58

	7			7	2	6	
	7	7	5		2		
1	5		5			6	
		5		3	5		
	4		6	1			4
5	1	6	6		1	4	2

▪ **Solutions** ▪

Page 59

Gwen should start by removing three apples from the bottom row, so that just one remains. Now there are rows with two, three, and one apple in respectively (which we'll write from now on as 2+3+1). If she makes any other move, Oli might win. But in this case, she is capable of forcing a victory for herself.

If Oli responds by emptying a row, there will be either 2+3, 2+1, or 3+1 apples left; or if not there will be 1+3+1, 2+2+1, or 2+1+1 apples. In the case of just two rows left then Gwen should reduce it to either 2+2 or 1+1 apples—preferring the latter state if possible, where she can then win on her next turn. In the case with three rows left, she should simply empty a row to leave either 2+2 or 1+1 apples.

Faced with any 1+1 situation, Oli must empty a row leaving just a single apple for Gwen to pick up and win with. If faced with the 2+2 situation, Oli will either empty a row, leaving a single row for Gwen to pick up both apples in and win, or he will leave 2+1 apples. Gwen can then take a single apple to leave 1+1, and again she will win on her next turn.

Page 60

She has three children: one with red hair, one with light-brown hair, and one with dark-brown hair.

▪ **Solutions** ▪

Page 61

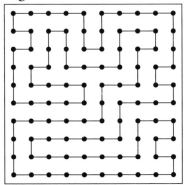

Page 62

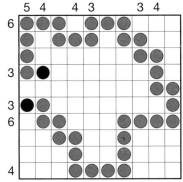

Page 63

Eight, if they all ran to time along the route, and potentially a ninth waiting to depart from the beach when she arrived, depending on their relative departure times.

Since the buses are hourly and she is four hours from the beach, there would have been four buses en route towards her at the point she departed—one every hour for the four hours before she left. Then, during her four hour journey, she should expect another four buses to depart from the beach. Since all the buses run the same route, she should pass all eight of these buses coming the other way.

▪ **Solutions** ▪

Page 64

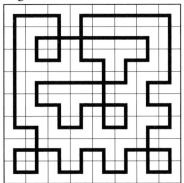

Page 65

Four coats. At the start of the game, Jon could take no more than two coats from the first rack in order to ensure that there was at least one coat of each color remaining on the rack. This could leave as few as one coat of a particular color.

He has at this point either taken two coats of different colors, in which case nothing needs to be done to complete the second stage, or he has taken two of the same color. In this second case, which would leave a single coat of one color on the first rack, Jon will need to be sure to pick enough coats to guarantee at least one of that color is returned. That means he'd need to allow for picking all six coats of the other two colors from the second rack, plus then one further coat to guarantee the color he needed to return. This would then leave on the second rack a total of four coats (i.e. the nine originally on it plus the two he transferred, minus the seven he then transferred back to the first rack).

▪ **Solutions** ▪

Page 66

Reference books cost six dollars, nonfiction books cost five dollars, and fiction books cost three dollars. These prices would be forced from the information given even if the constraint to keep prices to a multiple of one dollar was not present.

Page 67

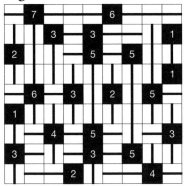

Page 68

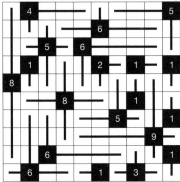

■ Solutions ■

Page 69

The numbers are being treated as hours on a twelve-hour clock, so the answer to 9 + 5 is two, since if you advance five hours from 9:00 you reach 2:00. Similarly, 7:00 plus six hours is 1:00; and 6:00 plus eight hours is 2:00; and 4:00 plus eleven hours is 3:00.

Page 70

The source of the information is a "double agent," which is the hidden message.

NATO phonetic alphabet code words (Alfa, Bravo, Charlie, etc.) have been hidden in the text, with exactly one hidden in each sentence of the letter. This is hinted at by the text "some kind of radio code" in the passage—the NATO phonetic alphabet is a radio code (i.e., a code suitable for reading over a radio link).

The letters indicated by the code words spell out "double agent" when read in order, with one word per paragraph. They can be found as follows:

> You have, to date, been a mo_del ta_sk force operative and we need your assistance with a serious, but sensitive matter. You will receive a series of important and confidential mem_os; car_ry on with your other work, but pay attention to concealed messages. Once the investigation has officially beg_un, I—for m_y own safety—will be moved to a secret location. For the duration of this operation you have been given the codename Co_bra, vo_ted for by your superiors. An "employee" who claims to work for us has managed to obtain confidentia_l imag_es and documents that pertain to top-secret missions. Th_e chosen_

▪ **Solutions** ▪

method of smuggling information from our premises seems to involve some kind of radio code.

The fin<u>al fac</u>ts of the matter are still unclear to us, so we need your help. We would like you to begin by looking into unusual transactions made in the company name at <u>golf</u> courses across the country. W<u>e cho</u>se you because we believe you stand the best chance of success, given your attention to detail. We are hoping to have the operation wrapped up by early <u>November</u>. Can you discover where the charla<u>tan go</u>t his information?

Page 71

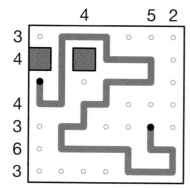

Page 72

X	O	X	X	O	X	X	O
O	X	X	O	X	X	X	O
O	X	X	X	O	X	O	O
O	X	O	O	X	O	O	X
X	O	X	O	X	O	X	O
O	O	X	X	X	O	O	O
X	O	O	X	O	X	X	O
X	X	X	O	O	X	O	X

168

■ **Solutions** ■

Page 73

The object was a blue die.

There is more than one color option for every object, so if Sid does *not* initially know what the object is then the object cannot be green or orange, as both of these colors can apply to only one of the objects—orange for the ball, and green for the toy block. Because Cassandra says she is sure that Sid does not know which object has the name on, the ball and toy block can be ruled out as possible options.

After Cassandra's first statement, this resulting elimination means that Sid knows that the object is either a die or a pen. Since he says he now knows which object has the name written on it, the color of the object must *not* be red—as it applies to both the die and the pen, and so wouldn't help him at this stage—so the color must be either yellow, blue, or purple.

After Sid's statement, Cassandra now knows the color. The only way Cassandra can know the color of the object at this stage is if she knows the object is a die, as it is the only object with only one color option left, and if the options were a yellow pen and a purple pen she could not be sure. This therefore reveals the correct object as a blue die.

Page 74

Fourteen drops will always guarantee them a solution, so they will never need more than this.

A naive method would start at the bottom floor and work up, which in the worst case would need a hundred drops. A maximum of fourteen drops is therefore a much more efficient method. To do this they start from the fourteenth floor. If it breaks from this height, they should go down to the first floor and check from floors 1-13, in ascending order, giving a maximum of fourteen attempts.

If the cup does not break from the fourteenth floor, they should go up

▪ **Solutions** ▪

to floor 27 and check from there, as if this caused the cup to break, it would still be necessary to check the twelve floors from 15 to 26, to give a maximum total of fourteen drops.

This process can be continued, starting at a gap of one less floor each time (due to the number of drops already made to reach that height)—at the 39th, 50th, 60th, 69th, 77th, 84th, 90th, 95th, and 99th floors. Following this strategy, the maximum number of drops needed to guarantee finding the floor from which the mug breaks is always fourteen, given the requirement that no more than two mugs can be broken.

Page 75

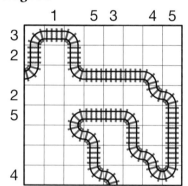

Page 76

No. The three possible changes in totals of each color when shaking hands are:

- Pink and green shake: pink -1; green -1; orange +2
- Pink and orange shake: pink -1; orange -1; green +2
- Orange and green shake: orange -1; green -1; pink +2

If you look at the difference in count of any pair of colors, say pink and green, then notice how the difference between those two colors changes after any of the possible color-changing handshakes:

- Pink and green shake: difference stays the same

▪ Solutions ▪

- Pink and orange shake: difference changes by three
- Orange and green shake: difference changes by three

No matter what happens, the difference between the number of pink and green lights (or any other color pair) changes only by an integer multiple of 3. Therefore, no color pair can ever have a difference of 0 because no initial difference is an integer multiple of 3.

Now if all the lights turned orange, both pink and green would need to be 0—which we know is impossible. Similarly for any other pair of colors, they cannot both be 0 for the same reasons, which in turn means that it can never be the case that all of the lights are a single color.

Page 77

Page 78

The chairman should reply, "You will not bring an appetizer or a main course."

If the guest then brought *nothing* to the party, that would mean the host's statement was true—but the guest had stated they would only bring nothing if the statement was *false*, so bringing nothing would violate that condition.

So, by her own rules, the guest must bring something to the party, but she cannot bring an appetizer or a main course as that

▪ **Solutions** ▪

would make the host's statement false—and a false statement means that the guest should bring nothing, which we already know would lead to a contradiction.

So the guest is forced to bring a dessert, unless she wants to break her own rules.

Page 79

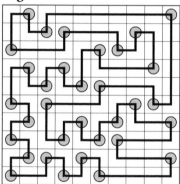

Page 80

1	40	30	15	14	29	46
⬇	⬇	⬇	⬇	⬅	⬅	⬇
33	41	31	10	32	11	48
⬇	⬇	➡	➡	⬅	⬇	⬇
23	42	22	17	27	28	43
⬇	➡	⬅	⬇	➡	⬆	⬇
25	6	7	9	26	8	47
➡	➡	➡	⬆	⬆	⬅	⬆
34	38	21	37	36	35	45
➡	⬇	⬆	⬅	⬅	⬅	⬆
2	5	20	16	4	3	44
➡	⬆	⬆	⬆	⬅	⬅	⬆
24	39	19	18	13	12	49
⬆	⬆	⬆	⬅	⬆	⬅	

∎ **Solutions** ∎

Page 81

The older brother will win again, and the younger will still lose.

The older brother—starting 10 meters behind the start line—has proved that he can run 100 meters in the same time that his younger brother can run 90 meters, as shown by the first race. With both brothers running at the same pace in the second race as they did in the first, the older will have run the first 100 meters of his 110 meters track in the same time it takes the younger brother to run 90 meters— meaning that they will draw level when they are 10 meters from home. The final 10 meters becomes a flat race between the two of them at this point, and given that they are running at the same speed as the first race then the results will be the same: the older brother will finish first.

Page 82

The woman's birthday is on December 31st, and the announcement is made on January 1st. This means that on the day of the announcement the woman is fifty-three, and she will turn fifty-five on the 31st December the following year. Two days ago, on the 30th December, she was still fifty-two. So they can both be correct, although it will be on the last day of next year that she can retire.

Page 83

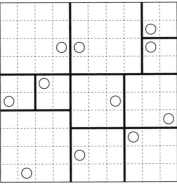

■ **Solutions** ■

Page 84

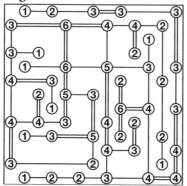

Page 85

He places five each of the remaining ten glasses into the smallest two boxes. He then places the smallest box inside the largest box, so that the largest box also contains those five glasses. His promise is therefore kept—at least in terms of the precise wording of his boss's instruction, if not its actual intent.

Page 86

Yes, they can leave this evening.

If the boatman always tells the truth then the whole statement is true, and the boat will leave this evening.

Similarly, if the boatman is a liar, then the boat will also leave this evening. This is because if he was lying then he would be one who did not always tell the truth, so on face value the condition would be false and the boat would not leave in the evening. However, because he *was* a liar, the boat *would* be leaving in the evening.

▪ **Solutions** ▪

Page 87

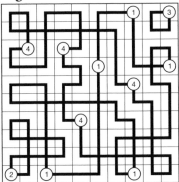

Page 88

1	2	●	2	●	2		●
●				3	●	2	
2		1		●			1
●	3	●	5	●	3	2	●
2		●	5	●			
●		3	●		2	2	
2		●	4		3	●	2
●	3	●		●	3	●	2

Page 89

The grapes can be arranged into a five-pointed star shape, with a grape at each point, and a grape at each central intersection of the lines joining these points, as shown here:

As such, the shape contains five rows of grapes, each with exactly four grapes in it.

■ **Solutions** ■

Page 90

The woman has thirteen grandchildren.

She has five children: three daughters and two sons. All three daughters have the same two brothers, and the two sisters are the other two of the three daughters.

Two of those children have two daughters of their own, which accounts for four grandchildren.

The remaining three each have three children, with each having two sons and one daughter (who is a sister to both sons). This gives nine additional grandchildren, taking the grand total of grandchildren to thirteen.

Page 91

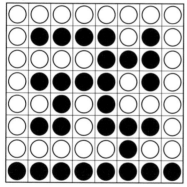

Page 92

Nine.

Taking nine socks from the drawer guarantees exactly four matching pairs, with one sock left over. All of the possibilities are as follows, where B is a black sock, W is a white sock, and the underlines show matching pairs.

- <u>B B</u> <u>B B</u> <u>B B</u> <u>B B</u> B/W
- <u>B B</u> <u>B B</u> <u>B B</u> B/W <u>W W</u>
- <u>B B</u> <u>B B</u> B/W <u>W W</u> <u>W W</u>
- <u>B B</u> B/W <u>W W</u> <u>W W</u> <u>W W</u>
- B/W <u>W W</u> <u>W W</u> <u>W W</u> <u>W W</u>

▪ **Solutions** ▪

Page 93

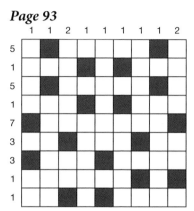

Page 94

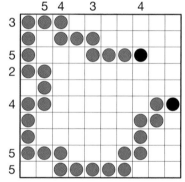

Page 95

Two coins.

If he leaves the house with two coins, then the first gatekeeper will demand half of his money—which is one coin. The gatekeeper will then give him one coin back, leaving the farmer to approach the second bridge, once again with two coins. This same process will repeat at every gate until he reaches the market, still with two coins.

▪ **Solutions** ▪

Page 96

The eastbound bus must be scheduled to leave three minutes after every westbound bus, so there are only fifteen minutes in every hour where the eastbound bus is the next bus (i.e. five buses an hour multiplied by three minutes). For the other forty-five minutes of the hour, the westbound bus will be the next bus. Therefore, assuming her arrival is truly random, then three times out of four she will end up going west.

Page 97

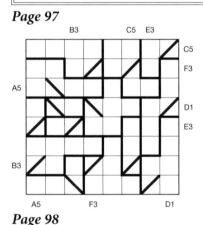

Page 98

It's a certainty.

Despite the title of this puzzle, no math is required. If the two journeys were happening simultaneously then at some point the journeys would cross, and at that point they would be in the same place at the same time. Given that both journeys began at noon and ended at 4:00 p.m., then at some point in those four hours the paths would inevitably cross—at that point and time they would be in the same location at the same time.

■ **Solutions** ■

What is not guaranteed is where the crossing spot would be. Given that presumably the mountaineer's pace is changeable, and his speed is unknown, the exact location of the crossing point of the paths cannot be calculated. Its existence, however, is guaranteed.

Page 99

0	3	1	5	0	2	2	0
4	6	6	5	2	3	3	3
5	2	2	1	4	6	1	5
1	6	5	6	1	6	4	2
3	3	1	0	3	2	4	6
6	1	4	0	0	2	4	0
4	1	3	0	4	5	5	5

Page 100

No—she cannot be right. If the two artists are left with exactly the same amount of paint after the mixing, then there must be exactly as much blue paint in the yellow pot as there is yellow paint missing from the yellow pot—and which must be in the blue pot.

The ratio of blue to yellow paint in the blue pot is exactly the opposite of the ratio of blue to yellow paint in the yellow pot, as no paint has been lost along the way—or in other words is equal to the ratio of yellow to blue paint in the yellow pot.

The lighter green may be caused by there being more yellow than blue in the original yellow pot, but not more than there is blue in the original blue pot.

▪ **Solutions** ▪

Page 101

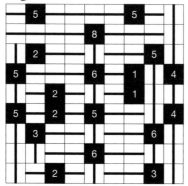

Page 102

Page 103

Three.

The key to the problem is that the models are told it is possible for *everyone* to work out what color their hat is, so there must be at least two of each color. If there was only one hat of a particular color then the model wearing it would have no way of being able to work out its color.

Any model who could see only one hat of a particular color could therefore deduce that her own hat must be that color too, given that there have to be at least two of each color, and leave the stage. This would then mean that any colors of hat left on the stage must be being worn by at least three models.

▪ **Solutions** ▪

Page 104

Before he left his shop, he noted the time on his clock that was now, after being wound, working again—but showing the wrong time. As soon as he arrived at the clock shop, he noted the correct time from the clock-shop clock. He also noted the time when he left the clock shop, so he knew how long he had spent there. When he then returned to his shop, he looked at the time now shown on his incorrect clock and subtracted the time it had shown when he left, so he knew exactly how long he had been away from his shop.

From this amount of time, he then deducted the amount of time he had spent at the other shop and then divided the remaining time in two, to calculate the time taken for one journey, since he had taken care to walk both journeys at the same steady pace.

Finally he then added this amount of time to the correct time noted when leaving the clock shop, and set his clock to this new, accurate time.

Page 105

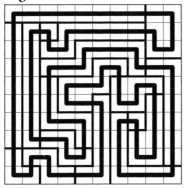

▪ Solutions ▪

Page 106

F	C	G	F	D	F	E	H
C	D	D	G	C	C	G	B
B	E	A	E	E	A	E	F
A	D	C	H	D	H	A	C
H	G	B	F	B	H	B	H
B	G	F	A	E	E	D	B
C	D	H	H	G	B	G	G
A	F	E	A	F	C	A	D

Page 107

First, she must take the cat over the bridge, then return to the original side while leaving the cat on the opposite bank. She can then bring the goldfish over the bridge and return with the cat back over to the original side. Once back at the start, she must leave the cat and take the dog over to the opposite bank. She can then safely leave the dog with the goldfish, and return to collect the cat, before crossing the bridge for the final time with all three animals then safely on the desired side.

She could also have swapped the order in which she had brought over the dog and goldfish, had she wished. The key requirement is that the cat is never left unattended with another animal.

Page 108

The North Pole.

A square house, built directly on the North Pole, would have walls and windows which all faced south.

For the exterior walk to be a possibility, the front door would have to be placed exactly on the North Pole. From here, a walk south, then east, and then north, would mean that the walker returns directly to the front door.

▪ Solutions ▪

Page 109

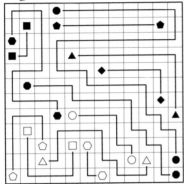

Page 110

He is engaged. The letter begins and ends with concealed "yeses," in the words "yesterday" and "goodbyes." In total, there are five concealed "yeses" in the text: yesterday, coyest, eyes, shyest, and goodbyes. In contrast, there are only four concealed "nos"—cannot, not, normal, and cannot (again)—suggesting that the overall response on balance is a "yes."

Page 111

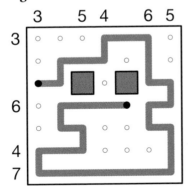

▪ **Solutions** ▪

Page 112

Bob blinked first, and Cat blinked last so is the winner.

The order of elimination is Bob, Dom, Amy, Eve, and finally Cat.

Page 113

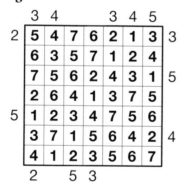

Page 114

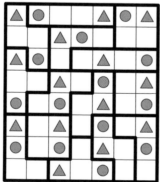

■ Solutions ■

Page 115

The seven herbs/spices are hidden in the note, written across words, with one per sentence. They have been concealed as follows:

- CHIVES: Sorry I've been out of touch—I've stopped picking up the phone, seeing as all I get is cold calls.

- BASIL: I never thought I'd be a local celeb, as I like to keep a low profile, but I'm suddenly popular.

- THYME: Everyone is trying to get hold of my secret blend of seven herbs/spices, and they're using stealthy means.

- CLOVES: The chronic love some people have for my blend is bizarre, but I'm entrusting the secret to you.

- CARDAMOM: Don't discard a momentous opportunity like this and, more importantly, don't tell a soul!

- MINT: I'm in town next weekend, so I can tell you in person then, but look hard enough and you'll find all the ingredients in this note anyway.

- DILL: It's tricky, though, and I'll be impressed if you can find all seven!

Page 116

The bunch of rhubarb would now weigh five hundred grams—half of its original weight.

We know that the portion of the rhubarb that is not water weighs ten grams, being 1 percent of the original weight of a thousand grams (one kilogram). If these ten grams remain constant after some of the water has evaporated, leaving the rhubarb at 98 percent water, then the ten grams must now form 2 percent of the overall weight. For these ten grams to be 2 percent of the weight, the overall new weight now must be five hundred grams.

■ **Solutions** ■

Page 117

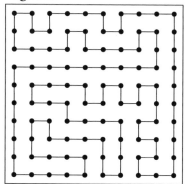

Page 118

Sal committed the crime.

Sam says that she is the liar, but if this is true then she has not lied (which she must, to be the liar), and if it's a lie then she cannot be the truth-teller either. So she must be the one who sometimes lies.

Sue says that she is not the one who sometimes lies, which is true, as we already know that Sam must be the one who sometimes lies. So Sue must be the truth-teller, since she cannot be the one who always lies because her statement is true.

By elimination this means that Sal must be the one who always lies, and therefore is the one who committed the crime.

Page 119

	A		D	B		D	
A	A	C		B		D	
C	C		D	A		B	B
	D		C		B	A	
A		A	B	C	D		D
B		B		D	A	C	C
	B	D	A		C		C
		D			D	C	

▪ Solutions ▪

Page 120

0	0	1	0	1	0	1	1
1	0	1	0	0	1	0	1
0	1	0	1	1	0	1	0
0	0	1	1	0	0	1	1
1	1	0	0	1	1	0	0
0	0	1	0	1	0	1	1
1	1	0	1	0	1	0	0
1	1	0	1	0	1	0	0

Page 121

Instead of flipping the coin once—which has an unequal probability of landing on either side—they should call either "heads then tails" or "tails then heads" and then flip the coin twice. If they get two heads or two tails they repeat the two tosses until they get two different sides. In this way they return to an even likelihood of either result.

Page 122

She should taste the contents of the jar labeled "blend," because then she is guaranteed not to find the blend of sugar and salt since she knows the label is wrong. Had she tasted any other jar she might have sampled the blend, which she might not have been able to identify since it has not been mixed. If, however, she tastes sugar, she can go ahead and use the "blend" jar to finish the dessert. If she tastes salt, then the sugar must be in the jar which says "salt"—since it can't be in the jar labelled "sugar"—and the "sugar" jar must contain the blend.

▪ **Solutions** ▪

Page 123

			4	6		5	
	2			6			
	1		6		3		
	3				1		5
1	3		5		12		7
	5				6		6
4		3	7	8		8	
		6					5

Page 124

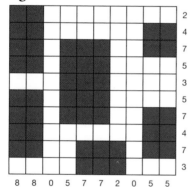

								2
								4
								7
								5
								3
								5
								7
								4
								7
								3

8 8 0 5 7 7 2 0 5 5

Page 125

Fifteen dollars.

To keep to the security rules, the box must be sent three times between the spies. The first spy will place the dossier in it and lock it with their own padlock, and send it to the second spy. When the second spy receives it they will add their locked padlock and send it back, with both padlocks attached. The first spy then removes their original padlock with their own key, and sends it to the second spy, who can take off the second padlock and reveal the contents.

188

■ Solutions ■

Page 126

The hidden items of jewelry are as follows:

- ANKLET: Before you run off and report this at the bank, let me just explain myself.

- RING: After I spent a year in Grandma's house, I noticed things were going missing:

- HATPIN: That pink scarf.

- TIARA: Her favorite cacti; a range of books.

- PENDANT: Most importantly, some top-end antique jewelry.

- BANGLE: So I took what jewelry was left and smuggled it out, wrapped it in her old turban, gleaning that it must have been a family member stealing her things.

- TORC: This doesn't count as a theft or crime—I'm sure of it.

- LOCKET: I've hidden the last eight pieces of jewelry, in the clock etched with Grandma's initials, at my place—but you can also find one per sentence.

Page 127

▪ **Solutions** ▪

Page 128

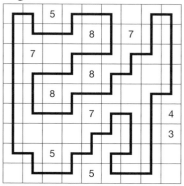

Page 129

No—the odds are two-to-one in Frederika's favor, as her bet was to guess the color of the hidden side of the notebook rather than what was written on the first page. It is true that the notebook on the desk cannot have "Admin" written on the first page, as it has one green side, so there is a fifty-fifty chance that the first page says either "Ideas" or "Meetings." But we don't know which way up the book is, so its sides may be blue+green or green+green, which means there are three possible chances for a green side and only one possible chance for a blue side. We can already see one green side, so there are two green sides and one blue side left as possibilities, giving odds of two-to-one that the hidden side is green.

Page 130

The shop assistant should divide the fifteen blocks of cheese into three piles of five blocks each. He should then place two of these piles on the scales, one pile on each side. If the scales balance, showing that both piles weigh the same, he will know that the lighter block of cheese is in the final pile. If one of the piles on the scales is lighter, he will know that the lighter block of cheese is in that pile. In either case, two piles of five blocks each can be put back in the bag. Once he has identified the pile containing the lighter block of cheese, he should place four blocks from the remaining pile of five on the scales, two blocks on each side. If they weigh the same, the one block left over is the lighter block of

▪ Solutions ▪

cheese, and only two comparisons would have been needed. If one pile is lighter, he should place the two blocks of cheese from that pile on either side of the balancing scale to determine which is the lighter block, giving a maximum of three comparisons.

Page 131

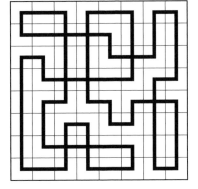